STRANGERS
A HISTORY OF NORWICH'S INCOMERS

Frank Meeres
2012

A NORWICH HEART PUBLICATION

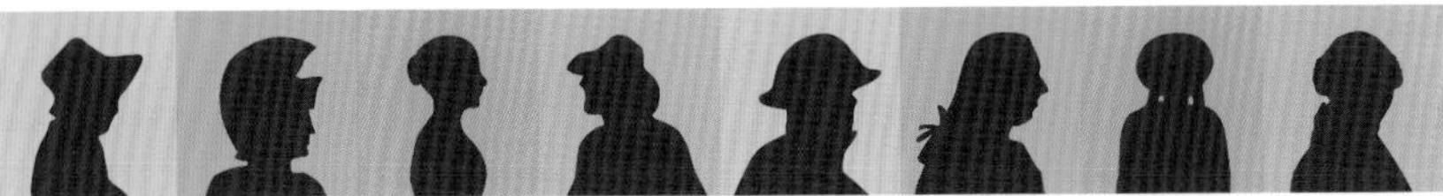

Opposite: Norwich in the 18th century: note the number of streets ending in '-gate'.

Published by Norwich Heritage Economic and Regeneration Trust (HEART)
Norwich HEART, The Guildhall,
Gaol Hill, Norwich NR2 1JS
www.heritagecity.org

Norwich HEART is a private, charitable company set up to act as an umbrella organisation for all the city's heritage. We strategically plan, regenerate, manage and promote Norwich's heritage and act as a best practice exemplar nationally and internationally for developing heritage as a vehicle for social and economic regeneration.

ISBN 978-0-9560385-4-8

Designed by Anne Reekie
Edited and project managed by Lindsey Roffe
Printed and bound in Great Britain by Swallowtail Print

The author has made every reasonable effort to provide correct and accurate historical information and to establish the copyright holders of all the photographs used in this book. This book is not a definitive account of all incomers to Norwich but aims to provide highlights on some of the incomers and their impact on the city over the years. Any errors or omissions are inadvertent. Anyone with queries concerning the content is invited to write to the author, c/o publisher.

All information in this book has been made in good faith and represents the author's professional judgement based upon information obtained from a range of sources. HEART cannot accept liability for the accuracy of the information and the consequent conclusions drawn from it.

Funded by

CONTENTS

ABOUT THE AUTHOR

Frank Meeres has worked for many years at the Norfolk Record Office. History is his passion: he has given a large number of talks and workshops on all aspects of the subject to both children and adults. He is the author of many books, including *The Story of Norwich (2012)*, and co-wrote a book on the history of Great Yarmouth which was given to every child in the town to celebrate the Millennium. He has a special interest in immigrants and refugees and has taken part in Refugee Week events in the city for several years.

INTRODUCTION

Norwich has always been a city that has welcomed incomers – immigrants and refugees: this book looks at the benefits that these newcomers have brought to the city over many centuries, and the part that they have played in creating today's city. Ancient incomers such as Romans, Saxons and Vikings have left their imprint in the form of street patterns and names, while the Normans created perhaps the three most iconic structures in the city – the Cathedral, the Castle and the Market Place. Norwich also had one of the largest Jewish communities in medieval England.

The city is known for the 'Strangers' who arrived from the Low Countries in the time of Queen Elizabeth I, and who at one time made up a third of the city's population.

There have been many immigrants from all over the world in the succeeding centuries, each group adding to the richness of city life. The book includes a walk around the city, illustrating many features where refugees and immigrants have left their mark upon today's urban landscape.

THIS BOOK TELLS THEIR STORY.

SHAPING 24

The production and printing of 'Strangers – A History of Norwich's Incomers' has been funded by SHAPING 24 (Strategies for Heritage Access Pathways in Norwich and Ghent). SHAPING 24 is a cultural tourism initiative linking together 12 heritage sites in Norwich that make up the Norwich 12 buildings, with 12 heritage sites in Ghent. This project was born out of the mutual desire to exploit the existing connections between the two cities. It seeks to promote and support the 24 sites, raise the profile of Norwich and Ghent as significant cultural heritage cities and increase awareness of the longstanding historical links between this part of England and the Low Countries.

Norwich – the city of Norwich is the most complete medieval city in Britain and, until the end of the 17th century, was England's second city with its wealth built on trading. Reminders of this remarkable heritage are everywhere with over 1,500 listed buildings within its walled centre, and it has more medieval churches than any other European city north of the Alps. Past trading links and a European influence are evident in the street-scape and architectural styles throughout the centre.

Ghent – the city of Ghent was one of the most important cities in Europe from the year 1000 to around 1550, second only to Paris in size and has played a prominent part in the history of Flanders. Today, Ghent is the capital of the province of East Flanders with a population of 250,000 and is both an historic and modern city. Using their beautiful assets together with innovative strategies, Ghent wants to be a pioneer in the area of social, economic, and ecological sustainability within fields such as culture and tourism.

Collaboration – Norwich shares many important aspects of economic, social and cultural history with Ghent going back centuries; the lives of the burghers, merchants and guildsmen in the two regions in the middle ages; the development of the wool trade in the 16th century; the establishment of trade routes; religious connections; and the importance of migration for the two cities – especially the settlement of Flemish workers in Norwich in the 16th century.

Historical Links – the common history, full of parallel features, reveals from time to time an amazing and largely unexpected continuity of interaction. Strong trading links between Norfolk and the Low Countries have existed for thousands of years and, indeed, this contributed to the strong links in general between the two. Low Country immigrants brought skills to Norfolk including cloth-making, leather-making, metal-working, shoe-making and brewing as well as many agricultural and horticultural skills. Goldsmiths and silversmiths from the Low Countries were resident in Norwich in the 16th century and the textile industry has long been connected between Norfolk and the Low Countries.

Modern day links – today, both cities also share a strong ambition for a pre-eminence in culture and the arts, especially in modern art. Norwich and Ghent are significant tourism destinations and their medieval origin is still recognisable in the lay-out of both city centres and by their historical monuments and the richness of their artistic patrimony. These two cities share a sense of cultural development and both strive to promote the distinctiveness of their city's heritage in a range of innovative ways.

FOREWORD BY MICHAEL LOVEDAY

What we have called 'A History of Norwich's Incomers' should, more appropriately have been called 'A History of Norwich People' because in many ways, as a microcosm of the English, what we are today is a result of 1,500 years of incoming. Firstly, our gene pool today is a composite of 1,500 years of integration with new comers. Look in the Norwich phone book and you'll see some very obvious 'new names' from the last hundred years that are now firmly part of Norwich – Valori (Italy) perhaps being one of the best known. Back over a century earlier we find Martineaus as 18th century French immigrants but 700 years before that, the Norman French gave us surnames like Abbs (a worker in an abbey), Amis (from 'friend'), and Archer (bowman, Clark (de Klerk), Johnson (Janssen) and Peterson (Peterssen) are products of Dutch immigration while Watkins and Wilkins are of Flemish origin.

Beyond the population itself we walk through 1,000 year old streets called Pottergate or Fishergate ('gata' being Danish Viking for street or way) or we relax in St Andrew's Plain (from the Dutch 'Plein'). On a Saturday we may quaff a pint of hopped ale (the Dutch introduced hops here) and then go and watch the Canaries – a term and a species introduced by Low Countries immigrants in the 16th century. Of all parts of England, with the possible exception of London, the Eastern Counties and Norfolk in particular, has been shaped by our interaction with Europe but, in the last half century, with the rest of the World.

It is appropriate, therefore that we have produced this book as part of a collaborative project with Ghent, in modern day Belgium, which not only has many cultural resonances with Norwich today, but was the birthplace of Jan van Gent, who we call John of Gaunt, son of Edward III and father of Henry IV – not a stranger to Norwich in the 14th century and a close contemporary of Sir Thomas Erpingham, local magnate and Captain of the English Archers at Agincourt.

Michael Loveday, Chief Executive,
Norwich Heritage Economic & Regeneration Trust

FOREWORD
BY BART DOUCET

Viewing the world as a set of long established nation states with very fixed national identities is a relatively recent mind set. Modern Belgium, for instance, has only been around since 1830. Equally, the status, character and culture of cities, like Norwich and Gent, has changed radically over time and what are regarded now as regional centres were, in their heyday, great European trading centres.

These two great cities saw themselves not as narrow, inward looking national entities but rather as vigorous members of an international community engaging not only in collaborative production and trade but also in cultural development, social change and even conflict resolution.

In many respects, Eastern England and Flanders, particularly during the medieval period, were more of a cohesive community than the England or the Low Countries of the time. Since then cultural, social and economic exchange has continued and even when Europe was divided by war in the last century, troops from Norwich engaged in the liberation of Gent.

Today the cities have many common resonances and only very recently, Norwich joined Gent in the UNESCO network of creative cities by achieving the accolade of the only English city to be awarded UNESCO Creative City of Literature status to sit alongside Gent as a UNESCO Creative City of Music.

Bart Doucet, Advisor,
Department Culture and Sport, Stad Gent

CHAPTER 1

Ancient Histories

The human race did not originate in East Anglia: everybody is an incomer. The first humans may have reached the area almost a million years ago, as shown by finds at Happisburgh on the Norfolk coast, but they moved south during the long periods when the area was too cold for anyone to survive – the so-called Ice Ages of ancient history.

Opposite: Bishop Herbert Losinga, the Norman bishop who built Norwich Cathedral, shown paying for the bishopric, in a painting in the Cathedral c.1200 (see pages 17 and 18).

Of course there were no national boundaries then: even the shape of the land mass has altered many times. There have been periods when 'Norfolk' was under the sea: this is when the flint that gives so many Norfolk buildings its character was formed on the bed of ancient oceans. At other periods, what is now the sea was land: animals and people could walk between 'Britain' and 'Europe'. The last Ice Age came to an end about 20,000 years ago and new groups of people reached the area. The genetic history of present-day inhabitants of Britain cannot be traced as far back as that, but it does go a very long way into the past. Stephen Oppenheimer, who has studied the subject, has concluded that two-thirds of English people have unbroken lines of genetic descent from south-western Europeans arriving in Britain over 6,000 years ago. Most of the remaining third are descended directly from people arriving between 6,000 and 3,000 years ago as part of long-term trading and immigration from north-western Europe, especially from Scandinavia.

ROMANS

The first written records of the history of what is now Norfolk begin with the Romans. In AD 43, when the Romans invaded Britain, Norfolk was a part of the kingdom of the Iceni, under Prasutagus, who became a client king of the Romans. The 'new town' of Venta Icenorum ('market place of the Iceni') was probably founded soon after: two miles south of the present city of Norwich, the Roman town at Caister is well worth a visit, with its imposing town walls. There was no Roman town where the city now stands. However, there were two Roman roads which crossed in the heart of present-day Norwich – near the *Hog in Armour* public house in Charing Cross. These roads can still be traced in great part. The north-south road ran past Caister, up Long John Hill, along Ber Street, crossed the river at Coslany and headed north along Oak Street and the Aylsham Road. The other road ran from the Midlands through the Fens. In Norwich, it ran along Dereham Road, Tombland Alley, across what is now The Close, over a ford where Bishop Bridge now stands, and up Gas Hill and Telegraph Lane towards Brundall. This route is now blocked by the bulk of Norwich Cathedral, itself the work of a much later group of immigrants to the city. The Romans who came to Norfolk were predominantly soldiers, men of many nationalities drawn from all parts of the Roman Empire: some of those at Burgh Castle near Caister-on-Sea, for example, are known to have originated from Swabia in Germany.

ANGLO-SAXONS

As the Roman Empire fell apart, a new wave of peoples invaded from North Germany and Denmark. These are the Angles, Saxons and the Frisians. However, they did not slaughter the British or drive them to the fringes of Britain as used to be thought, rather they slowly merged with them taking

A Saxon style round tower: St Mary Coslany, on St Mary's Plain off Oak Street.

Britain as a whole. The Anglo-Saxons are thought to have contributed just 5% to the gene pool.

The Christian church in East Anglia owes its roots to the work of incomers in the Anglo-Saxon period. It was first brought to the kingdom of East Anglia in AD 630 by King Sigebert, who had been converted while he was an exile – a refugee – in France. His first Bishop was Felix – a Burgundian by birth. A community of monks from Ireland was also brought in to help sow the seed of the new religion: they were led by Fursey and his brother Foillan and based in a monastery at Burgh Castle. There were later relapses into paganism but these immigrants began the long history of the Christian faith in the region: Saint Felix is now commemorated as the founder of the diocese of East Anglia in both the Anglican and Roman Catholic Cathedrals in Norwich.

The Anglo-Saxons have left memories in the form of place names – the name East Anglia itself is derived from them, and more local names like Coslany and Westwick are also Anglo-Saxon in origin. The word 'wic' means a trading place, and the name Norwich means 'the northern trading place': the word was probably first used for the settlement north of the river Wensum, later being used for the whole of the urban area.

Another legacy is the round tower. People in Norfolk are so used to round towers of flint attached to their churches that they do not realise how unusual they are: there are almost none in England outside East Anglia – but they are common in the parts of Europe from which the Anglo-Saxons came. There are several in Norwich, the most striking being those of St Mary Coslany and St Benedict, the latter standing alone since the rest of the church was pulled down after being bombed out in the Second World War. Although the actual buildings may date from shortly after the Norman

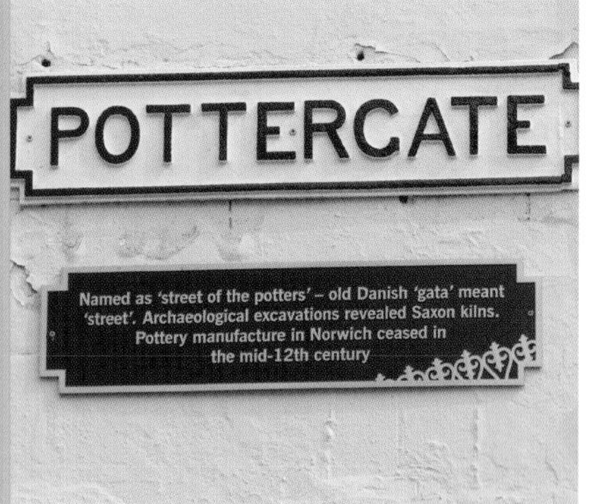

Above: Scandinavian street name: Pottergate.
Right: Vikings in Norwich: St Edmund murdered by Viking warriors, St Lawrence church.

Conquest, they represent part of the legacy of Anglo-Saxon culture in the city. Another characteristic form of Saxon architecture is 'long and short work': alternate vertical and horizontal stones forming the corner of a wall. To see this in the city today, look at the east end of St Martin at Palace church, where it can be seen clearly, a Saxon feature that has survived a millennium of change around it.

SCANDINAVIANS

A new wave of incomers arrived in the 9th century: Scandinavian forces, known to many as the 'Vikings', conquered the East of England after they defeated King Edmund in AD 869. The site of the battle is not known: this is traditionally said to have been at Hoxne, although a few authorities think it was at Hellesdon north of Norwich. The most likely spot of all is a meadow called Hellesdon in Bradfield St Clare close to Bury St Edmunds. King Edmund was killed after the battle: a medieval representation of his martyrdom can be still be seen in Norwich, carved in stone in the spandrel of the west door of the church of St Lawrence.

He is shown being struck by many arrows, the wolf which, according to the legend, guarded his head is also portrayed.

The Scandinavians were not just raiders, they had come to stay. The Treaty of Wedmore of 878 restricted them to the East of England, including Norfolk and Norwich. Present-day indicators of their importance include several more city place names. Most well-known is the street ending 'gate' as in Fishergate, Cowgate, Colegate and Pottergate, where the word does not refer to an opening but is the Scandinavian word 'gata' meaning way or street. Pottergate and Fishergate relate to the occupations practised on them, while Colegate is a personal name 'Cole's street'. There were other 'gata' in Norwich whose names show up on maps as late as the 19th century but have since gone. Sandgate, Skygate and Holgate all once ran from Ber Street down the steep hill to King Street, but are now lost under the post-war development of Rouen Road.

Two other Scandinavian words in everyday use as Norwich street names are Ber Street itself – Ber meaning ridge – and also Tombland. The word Tombland fascinated the boy hero of L P Hartley's novel *The Go-Between*, because he supposed it to imply the presence of graves. However, the name has nothing to do with tombs, in fact coming from a Scandinavian word for an open or empty space.

The Scandinavians were pagans at first but within a generation adopted Christianity. Their principal settlement was north of the river, probably centred around the church of St Clement, a popular church dedication among Danes (as in the well-known St Clement Dane in London). Other churches north of the river paid a portion of their tithes to Saint Clement centuries later, indicating that they had been carved out of the original parish as the number of inhabitants grew. Finds in the city reflecting the period of Viking occupation include a cross shaft with Scandinavian-style decoration found on the site of the church of St Vedast at Rose Lane, and now on display in the Castle Museum. The two groups lived together in the city in the later 9th and the 10th centuries: Brian Ayers, former County Archaeologist for Norfolk, has coined the term 'Anglo-Scandinavian Norwich' to describe the city at this time. There were a wide range of immigrants within this community. A skeleton found in an Anglo-Saxon cemetery on the site of the Mall shopping centre has been shown to have a distinct Romani DNA marker, the only example found in any English excavation of this period. The skeleton was that of a man: he had died young, some time between 930 and 1050 AD.

NORMANS

A new group of incomers, the Normans, arrived in 1066, and completely changed the urban landscape of the city. The three elements of this were the new Castle, the new Cathedral and the new Market Place, all still striking features of the city almost a thousand years later.

King William gave the earldom, city and castle of Norwich to Ralph de Guader in 1071. Ralph's father was originally from Brittany, while his mother was Welsh. His father had been in Britain in the reign of Edward the Confessor, so he can be described as a 'pre-conquest immigrant'. Ralph married Emma in 1075: she was the daughter of Roger de Breteuil, Earl of Hereford. According to the Anglo-Saxon Chronicle, the wedding feast

Falaise in Normandy. It was probably complete when King Henry I spent his Christmas here in 1121, as is recorded in the Anglo-Saxon Chronicle, but the inside of the Castle keep has been greatly altered since. Where the balcony now runs around the wall, was then the floor of the main apartments, and the large open arches now dominating the interior were then a solid wall. The main rooms were the

Above: The Norman Castle.
Right: The Norman Cathedral.

was actually celebrated in Norwich, although John of Worcester says it was in Exning. In any case, the men of Brittany – the Bretons – together with some English nobles, decided it was time to rebel against the Normans. However, forces loyal to the King forced the newly-married couple back to their stronghold in Norwich. Ralph then fled, perhaps to try to get help in Denmark, after which he returned to Brittany, his homeland. Emma was left to defend the castle, which she heroically did for three months: the historian F M Stenton says that, 'to her belonged all the honours of the war'. When finally forced to surrender, she was allowed to follow her husband to Brittany.

The present Castle followed, built over many decades; its design was influenced by castles at Brionne and

Great Hall, royal chamber and chapel with an ante-chapel next to it. On the west side were two service rooms and the latrines: they and the chapel in the south east corner are the two most obvious features from the medieval interior that can be seen today.

Opposite: Late 11th century Statue of Saint Felix, Burgundian-born founder of the diocese of East Anglia.

Norwich Cathedral was the work of another Norman immigrant, Herbert Losinga – born at Exmes in southern Normandy, his second name, which his father also had, may well come from the word Lothingaria, suggesting that the family had originated in the Low Countries. Herbert was educated at the Benedictine abbey at Fecamp, where he rose to become prior. He was brought to England by King William II, who made him Abbot of Ramsey. In 1090, he paid the King £1,000 to have himself appointed Bishop of East Anglia and his father Abbot of Winchester. His feelings of guilt about this led him to travel to Rome to obtain absolution from Pope Urban, and he is supposed to have built Norwich Cathedral as a penance. Paintings in the Cathedral dating from about a century after these events show Herbert handing over the money; Herbert, dressed as a Bishop, repenting; and the Cathedral itself. The Cathedral is a wonderful example of Norman architecture, especially the nave which has been little altered over the centuries (the vaulted roofs were built much later). The almost unique round chapels are probably based on those at Mehun-sur-Yevre in France. Herbert died long before it was complete and it was finished by his successor as Bishop, Eborard, another immigrant from Normandy. When it was finished, he retired – a most unusual thing for a medieval Bishop to do – and spent the last years of his life in his home country.

Both the Castle and the Cathedral were built, or at least faced, with stone brought by the Normans from Caen in their home territory, showing that the sea acted as a highway not as a barrier. The Castle was called 'la blanche fleur' (the white flower) in the Middle Ages from the whiteness of its Caen stone: however, this was replaced in the 1840s with the present stone, which comes from Bath.

Earl Ralph used the lands he held west of the new Castle to form a new borough: at its formation it had 36 French and six English burgesses. The older parts of the town suffered as a result of his rebellion, but the new borough flourished. The Market Place was moved from Tombland to the site that the present Market still occupies by City Hall. The Norman Market was larger, however, stretching from the present Guildhall to St Stephen's church. Tenements along the Market Place would have their short sides facing the Market and stretch a long way back from it: this pattern could be seen on the west side until the 20th century, when it was obliterated by the building of City Hall. It can still clearly be seen on the east side, where long narrow blocks of land run from the Market Place to the Great Cockey, now covered over by the street called Back of the Inns. A street pattern created by immigrants a thousand years ago determines the shape of today's streets at the heart of commercial Norwich.

The language expert Peter Trudgill stresses what a cosmopolitan place Norwich had become: 'After the Norman Conquest in 1066, Norwich itself, by now a rather sizeable town, must have been a very multilingual

Elizabeth Fry, née Gurney.
(Print after C. R. Leslie, 1835).

place. In addition to the original speakers of English and, for 200 years or so, Danish, there would have been obviously speakers of the newly arrived Norman French. The Normans also brought with them from the Continent large numbers of speakers of other languages, especially Flemish (Dutch) from the Low Countries and Breton (a relative of Welsh) from Brittany. It is astonishing to think of Tombland in Norwich alive with people speaking as many as five different languages'. However, the French and English inhabitants of Norwich soon merged into one community, a characteristic of the people of the city over the centuries. Richard of Devizes wrote in about 1190 that 'in Durham, Norwich and Lincoln you will hear scarcely any speaking Romance (French)'.

The number of Normans coming over to the city of Norwich can never have been more than 5% of the population, at the very most: Oppenheimer calculates that no more than 3% of the national gene pool is derived from Norman-French ancestry. Because they formed the elite, displacing Saxon noblemen, the names of this group of immigrants are mainly preserved among the upper echelons of society, those who 'came over with the Conqueror'. They include the Le Stranges or L'Estranges, best known as owners of Hunstanton Hall, and the Gurney family, said to descend from the Norman family of Gournay. The Gurney family have given many servants to the county and city including Elizabeth Gurney, the prison reformer, better known under her married name of Elizabeth Fry, and were founders of the great Gurney Bank, which later became part of the Barclays Bank empire.

THE HERB GARDEN OF
SOLOMON THE PHYSICIAN SON
OF ISAAC THE PHYSICIAN 1266
SAMUEL BEN ISAAC 1266
ISAAC THE LEEK (DOC
1243 · 1266
ELIAB B.
SELLARIA
WILLIAM DE BELTHAM
JOHN LE PALMER
1245 · 1258 · 1307
ELIAB BEN JACOB 1245
JUDAH BEN ELIAB 1253
ISAAC OF WARWICK
SADDLEGATE
OR WHITE LION
STREET
BENEDICT BEN ISAA
URSELL B. SAMPSON
ISAAC OF WARWICK
1253
JUDAH B. ELIAB
1259
SAMUEL BEN ISAAC
ABRAHAM B. MOSES 1255
STEPHEN ARBLASTER
WILL THE KNIFE SMITH

CHAPTER 2

The Jewish Community from the Norman Conquest to 1290

There was another group of immigrants in early medieval Norwich, the Jewish community. The chronicler William of Malmesbury says that Jews first came to England from Rouen with William the Conqueror, and there is no evidence for an earlier Jewish community in Norwich or anywhere in England. William's son, William Rufus, also encouraged them to come to Britain. There was certainly a Jewish community in Norwich by the reign of Henry II (1100-1135), and a taxation record from 1158 values the Norwich Jewish community as second in wealth only to that of London, and of about a third of its worth. Norwich was one of the half dozen cities where the Jewish community was ordered to centre its operations in 1194 – all deeds and contracts had to be registered and kept in a chest (archa) in one of these centres.

Opposite: A reconstruction by J P Chaplin of what is now White Lion Street showing the Jewish occupiers in the late 13th century.

The Jewish community was not large, perhaps numbering about 200 people at its height and declining to 50 or 60 in the decades before the final expulsion from England in 1290. The majority lived between the Castle and Haymarket, and this area was known to contemporaries as 'the Jewry': one reason to live in such a concentrated area was that the Jews might retreat into the Castle bailey for royal protection when they were threatened. Many people shop in Gentleman's Walk and White Lion Street today but few of them realise that they are on the site of the medieval Jewish community. At its heart was the synagogue, opposite the Haymarket.

The members of the community had a variety of occupations – we know of references in documents to several physicians, such as Isaac who lived on Saddlegate, the old name for White Lion Street. Another – Solomon – had a herb garden there. According to V D Lipman, the historian of the Norwich Jewish community, this is the earliest known reference in England to a private herb garden. Others were tradesmen, including cheesemongers, wine merchants and a fishmonger serving the rest of the community.

Agreement between the prior of Norwich Cathedral and Isaac son of Jurnet, drawn up in 1218.

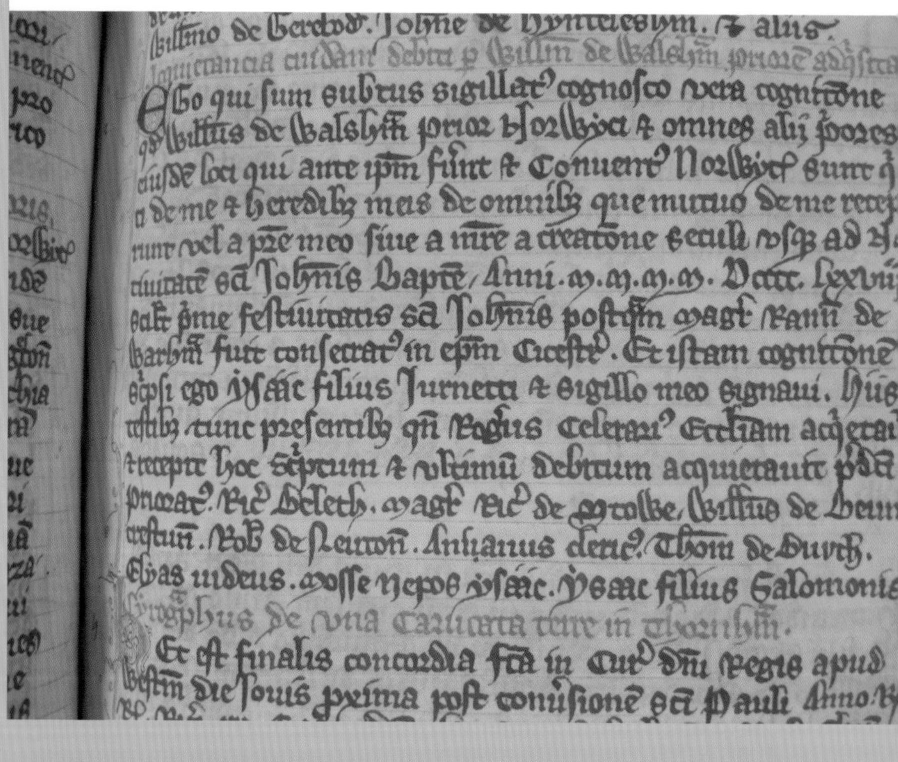

Reconstruction by J P Chaplin of the medieval Jewish synagogue.

Although most Jews lived in this area, it was not in any sense what would later be called a ghetto: people were free to enter and leave it as and when they wished, and not all Jews did in fact live there. There were cultural crossovers between the two communities: in the 1280s, two Norwich retailers, Roger de Lakenham and a man known as John 'the pastry maker' were charged with selling trefa. Although described as 'Jewish meat', this was actually meat not prepared according to Jewish methods and therefore rejected by Jewish butchers. It became illegal for Christians to buy such meat under a statute of 1267. The Norfolk Record Office has an agreement of 1290 between a Norwich butcher, Ralph Buteman, and the Jewish community concerning a wall between their property and that of the synagogue. The wall, twenty-four feet long, had been built partly on the property belonging to the Jews, and the Jews could have insisted that it be pulled down: instead they allowed it to stay, provided Buteman and any later occupier of the property was happy to maintain it.

Without the Jewish community, many of the greatest medieval buildings could not have been built: as Christians were forbidden to lend money at interest, it was only Jews who could provide the necessary funding for large-scale projects. They were involved with Norwich Cathedral: a charter survives relating to money owed by the prior of Norwich Cathedral to Isaac son of Jurnet. The charter is dated in the year 4978 of the Jewish calendar, which corresponds to 1218 in Christian dating. We know from a mason's mark that at least one of the masons who worked at Isaac's house also worked on the Cathedral Infirmary: links between the two communities were obviously close – and beneficial to Norwich.

THE JURNET FAMILY

The Jurnet family were the most well-known and the wealthiest members of the Jewish community. They did not live in the area known as the Jewry, but in a house in King Street later known as the Music House, and now as Wensum Lodge. The undercroft, or cellar, is the only surviving part of the house traditionally associated with Jurnet, but in fact owned by Jurnet's son Isaac, and by Isaac's descendants.

The first known owner was John Curry, who sold it to Isaac in about 1225: Isaac then obtained a licence to create a quay by the river here. Isaac died ten years later, in 1235, and the property was divided between his two sons, Moses and Samuel, with a further subdivision when Moses died in 1240. Some parts soon passed out of Jewish hands and the house itself was owned by Simon le Paumer by 1266, and possibly a decade earlier. The earliest part of the house, at right angles to the street, was constructed in the early 12th century: its five-bay undercroft still survives. In about 1175, the house was extended southwards along the street: only the lower section of two vaults and part of one of the piers of this aisled hall exist today.

Jurnet worked in consortium with his brother Benedict and with Jews in London as financiers: the group on one occasion in 1177 granted the enormous sum of 5,750 marks (almost £4,000) to the Crown, either as a loan or as an enforced gift. He lent money to Christian religious institutions with ambitious building programmes, such as Bury St Edmunds Abbey. Tradition says he married a wealthy Christian woman and they were forced to go abroad, and to pay a large fine on their return, but this legend is no longer believed. Jurnet died in about 1197 and his brother Benedict died in about 1204. Jurnet had at least two children, Isaac, already mentioned, and Margaret. Isaac was the wealthiest Jew in 13th century England: in the reign of King John he was fined the enormous sum of 10,000 marks for a legal infringement – it was to be paid at a rate of a mark a day for nearly thirty years!

COMMUNITIES

As we have seen, there was plenty of interaction between the Jewish community and its neighbours. Occasionally, anti-semitic feeling would flare up. The community came into the public eye following an incident that occurred on Easter Saturday 1144: the dead body of a twelve-year-old boy, a skinner's apprentice named William, was found on Mousehold Heath. The rumour spread that he had been murdered by the Jews in mockery of the Passion of Jesus: this is the first instance of such a claim in medieval Europe, an accusation to be made many times over the subsequent centuries. There is absolutely nothing to suggest that William was murdered by members of the Norwich Jewish community, and the authorities at the time gave the idea no support, the sheriff protecting the community within the Castle from anti-Jewish protests.

The communities settled down to almost half a century of peace, but anti-Jewish feeling was stirred up in the first year of King Richard I's reign (1189), because of his support of a crusade to the Holy Land. The community in Lynn was all but destroyed in a riot at the beginning of February, and the trouble spread to Norwich on the sixth, the community once more finding refuge within the royal Castle. There was more trouble between the Jewish community and citizens of Norwich in about 1230, some houses belonging to Jews becoming the victims of arson attacks.

In 1275, Jews were forbidden to lend money at interest and they turned their attention to transactions in corn and wood, many of which may well have been money-lending in disguise. At the end of the 1270s, national persecution of the Jewish communities in Britain was at its height: a large number of Jews throughout England were charged with coin clipping (cutting off the edges of coins to make additional coins) and a number were executed. They included at least sixteen in Norwich, the most well-known being Abraham son of Deulecresse, who was the most prominent member of the community at this time. He owned a block of properties beside the Haymarket which bore the name Abraham's Hall for another five centuries after his death. The Jewish community in Norwich came to an end in 1290, as a result of national government policy rather than because of any local feeling against them. All Jews in Britain were expelled by order of the King, and forced to leave for the Continent (a small number chose instead to convert to Christianity). Their property in Norwich as elsewhere came to the King – who, of course, sold it. The synagogue was destroyed by fire at about this time.

A CENTRE OF LEARNING

The Norwich Jewish community was a centre of learning: there were perhaps half a dozen rabbinical scholars here in the later 13th century, and the great scholar Berakhiah ha-Nakdan paid a visit to the city. It was also the home of a poet, one of only two from the early medieval Jewish communities in England whose voice is still known (the other is a poet from the London community Jacob son of Judah, from whom three minor works survive). There is a manuscript in the Vatican Library of poetry written by one Meir son of Elijah. Several are in the form of an acrostic, one of which reads: "I am Meir, son of rabbi Elihu, from the city of Norwich which is in the land of isles called Angleterre. May I grow up in the Torah of my Creator and in fear of him: Amen, Amen, Amen, Selah." Nothing at all is known about the poet: one of his poems may refer to the expulsion of the Jews from Britain, in which case he was presumably one of those forced to leave in 1290, but the poem does not specifically refer to an expulsion across the sea:

Forced away from where we dwelt.
We go like lambs to the slaughter.
A slayer stands above us all.
We burn and die.

Over five centuries after they were written, the works of this poet and refugee have been made available in English for the first time, a project originated by local journalist Keiron Pim and assisted by translators Ellman Crasnow and Bente Elsworth of Norwich. Appropriately, the latter are both immigrants themselves – Crasnow was born in South Africa, Elsworth in Denmark.

CHAPTER 3

Links in the Middle Ages

Norwich was the largest town in Britain apart from London throughout the Middle Ages: much of its wealth came from wool. The skill of weaving is said by tradition to have first been brought into Norfolk and Norwich by Flemings. An early mention of Flemish settlers in the weaving business is in a Parliamentary petition of 1315 relating to a disagreement about the size of the units in which cloth was sold. There are many other examples of links in the weaving industry between Norwich and the Low Countries.

Opposite: 'Green Man' boss in the cloister at Norwich Cathedral, carved by a Dutchman named Brice.

In 1311, four Norwich citizens and two Lynn men sold wool worth £1,000 in Bruges, then went to Lille fair and bought £1,500 of spices, cloth, wax and other goods for the return trip: these are enormous sums of money for the Middle Ages, the equivalent of perhaps half a million pounds today. A man named John Kempe came to Norwich from Flanders before 1331 to teach his system of weaving: he is probably the same man as the John Kempe de Gaunt [Ghent] mentioned in a Norwich tax list of the time. The city records include a copy of the letter patent issued by King Edward III in 1352. It welcomed foreign cloth workers into his kingdom to 'come to the same realm and lands both safely and securely under our protection and safe conduct and should dwell in the same realm and lands where they might wish, and that we should grant so many and such liberties to the same workers as should be sufficient for them so that they might come here the more freely'.

King Edward was married to a Flemish princess, Philippa of Hainault, so it was natural that the interests of the two lands should be closely linked. Two of their children were born in her home territory, Lionel of Antwerp and John of Gaunt: it is a pity that the name Ghent has been anglicised to Gaunt as it means many people are unaware of his foreign birth. Gaunt was a friend to Norwich: when he visited the city, every freeman in the city was ordered to turn out to honour him. Norwich supported Gaunt's son Henry in the dispute between him and Richard II to the throne of England at the end of the 14th century. After Henry did become King, he rewarded the city with a charter that made Norwich a county in its own right – a status it was to hold until 1974.

TRADING LINKS

There were many trading links between Norwich and Europe, and some of the merchants became short or long term immigrants to the city. A trade agreement survives from 1286 between the Norwich authorities and six merchants of Amiens and Corbeil in France dealing in woad, 'ashes' and weld: woad is a blue dye which is also used as a fixative for other dyes; weld was cultivated for its yellow dye; the ashes were perhaps carbonate of soda used as the alkali in dyeing. Three of the men had the 'surname' of le Mouner – Nicholas, Peter and Ralph, probably one family. The others were Peter and Firminus Cokerel and John Feuyerter.

We know where at least one of these immigrants lived. Historians William Hudson and J C Tingey tell us the story: 'In the Court Roll for 1287, the year after that in which the agreement was made, one of them, Peter le Mouner, is seen to have purchased a house in Norwich, and he appears to have resided in it with his house and family until his death, which occurred about 1330. This house was on the east side of the way just over Fyebridge, and therefore had the river on the south and Fyebridge Quay opposite. A most convenient situation if it was customary to bring the woad and other goods by water to that spot, for the merchant would be able to observe the arrival and departure of his boats without leaving his dwelling'.

When a boat upset at Cantley in a storm in 1343, its cargo included salt, sea coal, iron from Sweden and boards from Riga in modern-day Latvia. Forty people drowned in the tragedy and the boat was said to have been overcrowded, a tragic echo of the stories of immigrant 'boat people' in later centuries including the present one: however, in this case we do not know if any were immigrants seeking new homes. Lists of dues collected on goods unloaded on the Norwich staithes in 1378 again included board from Riga, and also herrings from Skane in southern Sweden and iron from Spain.

Many other examples can be given of imports into Norwich from abroad during the Middle Ages. Black salt, brought in on Dutch ships, probably originated in the Loire Valley and was carried first to the Low Countries and then onto Britain. Fine salt, either boiled down in Holland or obtained from Low Countries' peat, was also imported, valued by customs at twice as much as black salt. Other imports included wax, sandals and cotton; basins, pots and pans – mentioned from 1400, perhaps the first influx of Dutch salt-glazed stone-wares, much superior in strength and less porous than native English pottery. Another import was the plant of madder: used as a dye, it was grown in Zeeland and gathered in autumn. Its sale in the city has given rise to the Norwich place name of 'Maddermarket'.

The merchants organising these shipments might live on either side of the North Sea, or perhaps have houses on both sides. William Heynsser, who owned the Norwich-based ship, the Christopher, in the later 14th century was probably a Dutch immigrant. John Asger, who was mayor of Norwich in 1426, is described on his brass in St Lawrence's as 'once a merchant of Bruges': his son was born in that city. Asger senior was there when he was chosen as mayor, an entry in the city Assembly books recording that the expenses of travelling to fetch him back were to be paid by the community. Another important trader of the time was Robert Toppe; he used Dragon Hall as his showroom, displaying wares brought up-river and coming from all over the known world, usually via the Low Countries. There is a brass from 1500 of a Dutch merchant in St Peter Mancroft church: it was later turned over and re-used as a memorial to Sir Peter Reade!

MEDIEVAL INCOMERS

Apart from weavers and merchants, there were many other incomers in medieval Norwich, contributing to city life with their varied talents, including a painter and several goldsmiths. Giles 'the Fleming of Bruges, painter'; is mentioned in a document of 1293. The first known record of a goldsmith in Norwich is a man named Salomon who possessed land in St Peter Mancroft in 1141: he was probably a member of the Jewish community. In the 14th century, there were two wealthy goldsmiths in the city whose names suggest they were immigrants. Henry de Brabant lived in St Peter Mancroft and was involved in seventeen property transactions between 1304 and 1333. John de Norwege [Norway] was buying and selling property in the city between 1317 and 1323. In 1494, Thomas Goldsmyth, described as 'alien and goldsmith', paid five marks to be made a freeman of the city, as did two Dutchmen, Peter Peterson and Gerard Johnson, in the following year. The well-known 16th century goldsmith Peter Peterson is said to be the grandson of this Peterson.

REFUGEES

There was an influx of refugees from the Netherlands in Norfolk and Norwich in the 15th century. Some were economic refugees and others fleeing from persecution: it was a time of great upheaval in their own country, some natural and some man-made. In 1420s Holland alone, there were terrible floods in 1421 and 1422, a civil war in 1425 and a peasants' revolt in North Holland in 1426. These disasters caused devastation to villages and towns, and many refugees made the short trip across the sea to Great Yarmouth, and from there up-river to Norwich. They included tailors, smiths, glass-makers and even an organ-maker, Arnold Dutchman. They also included two hat-makers, apparently bringing a new trade into Norwich. We know the names of many of these people because of the actions of the British Government – they 'registered' them by entering their names on the patent rolls – and (in a 21st century touch) they were also expected to swear an oath of allegiance to the English Crown. As in the 20th century, immigrants from countries with whom England happened to be at war were especially closely watched.

The 'nations' from which these immigrants came are not always places seen on present-day maps. Immigrants living in Norwich in 1436 had come from a wide range of 'countries' – Holland, Zeeland, Brabant, Hainault, Gelte, Utrecht and Germany, only the first and last of which we would regard as countries today, and even their borders are very different to the mid-15th century countries. Those described as 'from Brabant', for example, came from cities like Brussels, Antwerp and Louvain. The Germans came from a range of cities, including as far away as Hamburg and even Danzig. Some of the residences of immigrant families have been uncovered by archaeology, recognisable by their different tools and utensils – such as the frying pan, apparently brought in by Flemish settlements in the early 15th century.

We can still see the craftsmanship of at least one immigrant in the Cathedral cloisters. Stand in the south-west corner of the cloister, by the door leading up some steps to the new refectory. Look up at the carved stone bosses. Can you see the face of a man peeping through leaves? This is known as a Green Man. We know who carved this face in the stone: it was a man named Brice, described in the records as 'Dutchman'.

In 1416, he was paid 4s 8d (about 23p in today's money) for his work: it took him two weeks to carve.

The Dutch also brought what has become England's most traditional drink – beer. Before their arrival, the English drank ale instead – made without hops, not so strong and harder to keep fresh. There are many references to Dutchmen and beer in the archives of the city. In 1469, John Petirson, Dutchman and beer brewer, was fined for sending victuals and candles overseas, amongst other offences. John Heynes, a Dutchman, was fined in 1472-3 because his barrels of ale did not contain the legally-required quantity of 30 gallons.

In the days before documents like passports and identity cards it was not always clear what 'nationality' a person had. In 1496, Newell Addurge, described in the record as a Frenchman, paid 26s 8d to be sworn in as a citizen. A note in the margin beside his name reads 'Dutchman'. In the same year a 'Frenchman' called Andreas Kenetton, purse-maker, was admitted to the freedom 'if he be not Scottish'. A note in the margin beside his entry reads 'He is a Scot': Kenetton had failed this particular immigration test.

SKILLED WORKFORCE

Immigrants who had skills to teach were always especially welcome, and were sometimes 'head-hunted', such as the hat-makers and russell-weavers who were brought into the city in 1542. Documents of the time record that some citizens of Norwich 'have invented and begun the craft of hat-making within the same city which they can now make as well and as good as ever came out of France or Flanders or any other realm, whereby they have honest livings and set many persons, poor people and children of the said city, to work'. The words "came out of France and Flanders" have been crossed out and replaced with "were made in" so that the origins are no longer obvious. A list of seventeen Frenchmen in Norwich in the 1540s includes three who are described as hatters – John Glasier, Andrew Tiphany and John Jevort. Two others – Nicholas Tiphany and Peter Oreng – are not given any occupation, but as they lodged with an English hat-maker, they can be included among the immigrants bringing this new skill into the city.

Russell-weaving was introduced at about the same time, and by many of the same men who had begun the hat-making industry. Russells had previously been made abroad but using Norfolk wool: the name may come from Rijsel, the Flemish name for Lille. Thomas Marsham, the mayor, with other aldermen and merchants, had looms made and brought strangers from beyond the seas to train Norwich people in the skill.

ROMAN CATHOLIC CHURCH

The Roman Catholic church united the whole of western Europe in a single faith and a single liturgical language – Latin. This meant that people could travel in search of promotion, or to be of service. One of the Bishops of Norwich in the early 13th century was Italian, Pandulph. He took the salary and even came to visit his diocese on one occasion! A century later, groups of friars came to the city, among them followers of the Italian Francis of Assisi and the Spaniard Dominic. They were dedicated to lives of extreme poverty, and, although the original seed was from Europe, many English people chose to join such groups. They tended to lose their ideals of poverty over the centuries, as indicated by the grandeur of The Halls complex in Norwich today, the home of the Black Friars. Friars were internationally organised orders, as the story, or legend, of Peter of Candia illustrates. Supposedly, he was an orphan born in Crete in about 1339: 'a homeless beggar-boy in a Cretan city, knowing neither parents nor relations', (as he is called in one biography), he was brought up in a Franciscan friary on the island. He joined the Order himself, firstly in Padua and later coming to the Norwich Franciscan friary as a young man. He went on to study at Cambridge University, and later lectured at universities throughout Europe. In 1402 he became Archbishop of Milan. This was at a time when there were two rival Popes. A council in 1408 met to sort this out, it deposed both the rival Popes and elected Peter as the new Pope. He took the name Alexander V, but the other two Popes both refused to resign, so that for a time there were three Popes! Alexander was recognised by England, and by several other countries, but not by others. He showed his interest in England by issuing a formal condemnation of the teachings of John Wycliffe. He died in Bologna the following year, so suddenly that there were rumours that he had been poisoned by one of his rivals. He is officially regarded as an 'anti-pope', but some authorities prefer to call him a 'Conciliar Pope' as he was elected by a council of the church. This story of his life was universally believed for five centuries, being recorded on the 19th century inscription on his tomb in Bologna. Recent research has cast some doubt upon his true origins: however, he was certainly from an Italian background, and so can be counted as one of Norwich's most distinguished immigrants – and he is the only Pope with a direct link to Norwich.

Pope Alexander V, Italian-born immigrant.

Like religion, medicine also transcends national boundaries and we have seen that there were physicians among the medieval Jewish community. Another important figure in the world of medicine was Thomas Phaer, born in Norwich of Flemish parents in 1510. His *Book of Children* was the first book of child medicine written in England. He did not live in the city of his birth as an adult, spending most of his life in Wales and becoming a Member of Parliament for Cardigan.

THE ISBORNE FAMILY

One immigrant family for which we have a lot of incidental detail is the Isborne family. In 1534, Nicholas Isborn 'goldsmith alien' was admitted to the freedom: he was also sworn into the guild of St George, paying £5 for these privileges. Nicholas Isborne's house was at the corner of London Street and Redwell Street. He died in 1555, and is buried in St Michael at Plea, as is his wife Katherine, who died in 1568. They had at least two children, Anne who died in 1570 and Valentine, to whom Nicholas left his tools. Valentine became apprentice and servant to another immigrant goldsmith, Zachary Schulte who had purchased his freedom in 1548. In 1551 he was before the courts when Katherine Grey 'late servant of Zachary Schulte goldsmith' complained that she was with child by him. Valentine presumably disentangled himself from Katherine as in 1556 he married Alice Albone in St Michael at Plea church. He was before the courts again in 1562 in what a detective writer might call 'the mystery of the blue sapphire'. He accused his servant, Robert Cullington of stealing a blue sapphire worth 100 shillings – at least £1,000 in today's money. Cullington emphatically denied having it and the case against him was dismissed: the fate of the jewel is not known.

Valentine Isborne ran into financial problems later in the decade: in 1568 the mayor's officials took the tools from his shop windows in distraint. He is listed in the 1570 Census of the Poor: we are told he and Alice were both 38 years old. He was a goldsmith (presumably more or less unemployed, as he would not otherwise be in the census), she knitted and 'helped others', that is, did general chores like washing. They had four children aged 9, 7, 5 and 2 who are described as 'idle', perhaps implying that the older ones were of an age where they might have been making some contribution to the family income. The whole family is classed as 'Pore', but they did at least own the house in which they lived. The youngest child, Robert, died in 1579 aged ten. The other three married, all using the nearby church of St Michael at Plea for their wedding and the baptisms of their children. The eldest, Laurence, married Joan Tennant and had seven children between 1583 and 1601, most of whom died as infants: however, at least one of his daughters, Olive, grew up to marry Robert Lad in 1607 when she was nineteen or twenty. The other brother, Augustine, married Mary Narborough and they had at least three children. The fourth child of Valentine and Alice was a daughter, Dorothy; she married Thomas Moody in 1603. The people whom the Isbornes married were all English: clearly they had become very much part of the city community in Norwich. At what point did a family like this come to regard themselves as 'of Norwich' rather than as immigrants?

CHAPTER 4

The Strangers

The word 'Stranger' really means anyone who was not a member of the city community, and could apply to English people from outside Norwich as well as to people of other nationalities. It was only in the 16th century that the word became applied to a particular group of incomers, Dutch- and French-speaking families fleeing from religious persecution in the Low Countries: these are the people we now think of as the 'Strangers'. The French speakers among them are often also called 'Walloons'.

Opposite: Reverend John Elison, along with his wife Maria (see page 54), had the distinction of being painted by Rembrandt in 1634. Photograph © June 2012 Museum of Fine Arts, Boston.

THE LOW COUNTRIES

The first groups of 'Strangers' were invited in by name, for reasons explained in a letter by Thomas Sotherton, mayor of Norwich:

> *'By reason that the commodities of worsted making is greatly decayed, by the which many citizens both merchants and artisans that before that time had (of the gain thereof) their whole livings. And great number of poor of the City were set on work, by spinning, weaving, dyeing, calendaring and shearing the said cloths, which now were out of estimation and vent, that the makers and workers thereof in all the exercises aforesaid, were fain to give themselves to other exercises and trades to maintain their families which was nothing so profitable hereby people became poor, many left their houses and dwelt in the country, that the houses decayed for lack of farms and that they were let at small prices, and the city like to decay if prudent policy did not assist the same. And after many consultations and devices, what trades might be practised to redress this poor state; was given intelligence that divers strangers of the Low Countries were now come to London and Sandwich and had got licence of the Queen's Majesty to exercise the making of Flanders commodities made of wool, which strangers come over for refuge against the persecution then raised against them by the power of the Duke Alva, principal for the King of Spain. And because the poor here might be exercised in their spinning and wool work a motion was made to Thomas, then Duke of Norfolk, then lodged at his house in this City, that at his return to London he obtained of the Queen's majesty, who of her gracious goodness and merciful clemency, having compassion of the poor state of this her highness' city, did tolerate and admit to be and inhabit within this her highness' city of Norwich thirty master workmen, to have either of them ten servants, to exercise the making of these commodities, with warrant to the mayor and citizens to permit them so to do.'*

Queen Elizabeth issued a public letter on 5 November 1565, which referred to 30 Dutchmen (not specifically mentioning any Walloons) but named only five of them – John Powells, William Steene, Henry Clercke, Peter van Brugen and Bartholomew Johnson. Only three of these were included in the actual invitation seven months later – Clercke and Johnson presumably decided against coming to Norwich, or may have died in the interim. The invitation named thirty men – 24 Dutch speakers and six Walloons – and allowed each to bring up to ten family members, a term which would have included apprentices and servants, so that a maximum of 300 people were involved.

Work by Raingard Esser has shed further light on the thirty incomers. At least half had already been in England for a time, living in the communities of Dutch exiles already established in

Sandwich and London, from which they were in effect 'poached': the others were living overseas at the time of their invitation into Norwich. Not all were involved exclusively in weaving: Romaine Dedecre was a surgeon, as well as a sayeworker (a fine-textured cloth worker), Thomas Bateman a merchant, Robert Goddarte a dealer in cloth and bays, George Vamboute, from St Jans-Kappel, a teacher and preacher as well as a wool comber. He was one of three of the men who were in trouble in the home country for sectarian activities: the other two were Peter Waells, a farmer from Houtkerke, and Paschal Clarebote, a wool comber from Winnezele.

Although the first 'Strangers' were invited in, regime change in their home country led them to be followed by many hundreds of others, refugees in the full sense: the Spanish forces of the Duke of Alva reached Brussels in August 1567 and there was immediate persecution of those of Protestant beliefs. The historian Pieter Geyl says that 'never was a nation subjected to a reign of terror with more calculated deliberation or more systematic persistence'. The Duke himself wrote at the time, 'everyone must be made to live in constant fear of the roof breaking down over his head'. It is no surprise that many fled: over 60,000 people are said to have left the Southern Netherlands under Alva's rule. Many went to the Northern Provinces or to Germany, but others preferred the journey across the sea to England – and many found their way to Norwich.

These people suffered the kinds of experience familiar to refugees throughout the centuries. One of these was the family of Janus Gruter, born at Antwerp in 1560, whose family fled to Norwich when he was a small boy. His mother later wrote a letter to a friend, describing the flight. They arrived first at London:

> *'Then we journeyed 90 miles with four children for two months by land on a waggon and came to a town called Norwich where there were about 1200 Flemings and among them all not one person that I had ever seen before. We did not know what to do to earn our living there. The trade was the spinning of wool and preparing of bays, in which we had no skill, so we had to join together with other people and bought wool and supplied the poor people with wool and took bays in exchange and sent them to London to sell them there. There we chanced upon a merchant who, when the day for payment came and we thought to have our money, was bankrupt, and £450 Flemish was lost; that was our first welcome. The second was that the same man who was in partnership with us left England secretly to cross to Flushing with £300 sterling and on arrival at Flushing he jumped into the water for fear of the Spaniards who came alongside, and sank with all the money and never came up again. And so we lost that too. I leave you to imagine how we felt then, but the Lord be praised for the grace that he gave my dear husband. I never saw*

him even sigh about it, he only said, 'The Lord gave it and he has taken it away again, blessed be his name'.

Janus Gruter went on to Cambridge University, and later became one the greatest literary figures in the Europe of his day.

Some of the more fortunate refugees brought money with them but others must have needed immediate financial support such as Nicholas de Linne and his wife who arrived with eight children. Some women came on their own such as Barbara Moded, the daughter of a preacher, Herman Moded, who came over from Antwerp. A whole group came over from Dieppe in the winter of 1567, having fled from persecution in East Flanders. They included just one man, Jacob de Poultier who came with his wife and two daughters. Others in the group were Maria Faber, the widow of Jean Faber, who brought her seven children with her; the unnamed wife of Pierre des Passetts who came without her husband but with their three children, and two other widows Jean Clapettia and Jeanne le Dente. These refugees must have been in a desperate state to cross to a new land in the depth of winter. Other refugees may have been able to bring more possessions with them. When incomer Vincentiana Herjtes died, her worldly goods included a Flemish cloak, a Dutch hat and a Dutch hood – had she brought these with her from her homeland?

LETTERS HOME

Some of the refugees wrote to friends and family in their homeland: these letters, once in Ypres Town Hall in Belgium, were destroyed in the First World War, but transcripts survive and make fascinating reading. Some examples are given here:

Pawels de Coene to his wife, 21 August 1567. He sends her a barrel of herrings, which she is to sell to provide means for her journey: he warns her that the journey is becoming more dangerous every day and hopes to rent a house so that all will be ready for her when she comes. His wife and five children were in Norwich by August 1568.

Clais van Wervekin, hat-maker, to his wife in Ypres, 21 August 1567. 'You would never believe how friendly the people are together, and the English are the same and quite loving to our nation. If you come here with half our property, you would never think of going to live in Flanders. Send my money and the three children. Come at once and do not be anxious. When you come bring a dough trough for there are none here. Know that I await you and doubt me not; send me Catelynken, Saerle and Tonyne. Bring also our long hooks to hang your linen cords on. Buy two little wooden dishes to make up half pounds of butter; for all Netherlanders and Flemings make their own butter, for here it is all pigs' fats'. This is an early example of a refugee finding the diet of his new home not entirely as he would wish.

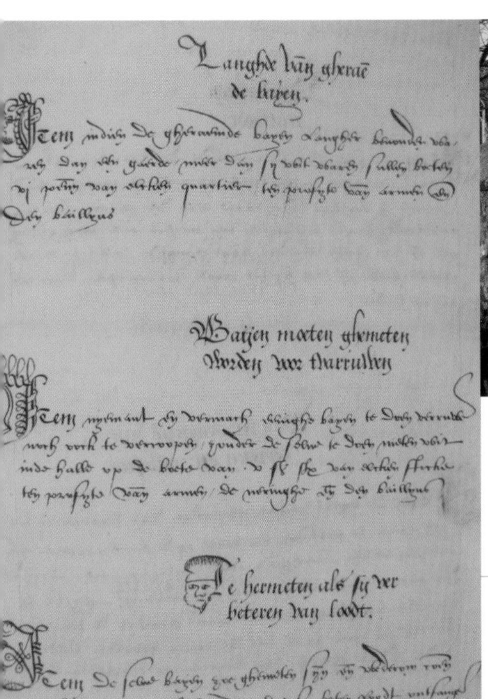

Langhde van gheraē
de baijen.

Baijen moeten ghemeten
worden voor thaerulven

De hermeten als sij ver
beteren van loodt.

Left: Book of Orders in Dutch.

Above: A Norwich Plain: the word has come to us from the Dutch language.

Andries and Anna van der Haghe, brother and sister, to their parents in Ypres, 28 August 1567. They appeal to their father, mother, brothers and sisters to come to England and not to wait any longer. They inform their father that two of his debtors, Pieter Keerle and Steven de Mol are at Norwich and waiting to settle up with him. 'I and my brother will supply you with what you require here as weaver, for there is a great trade doing… Will you greet Lieven van de Walle and his wife for us, not forgetting our grandmother, uncles and aunts and all our other friends'. They offered practical advice to fellow refugees: 'We pray you, when you get to Nieuwport, take the vessel that comes to Great Yarmouth, for otherwise you would have a day's more voyage. For when people come to Sandwich, it costs double for they must then go on to Norwich. I have a gold coin. I would like to send it in the letter but when you come to Norwich, I will give it to you, for then you may have nothing in your pocket: when you come to Norwich you shall have gold'. More than one of the letters mentions that it was being sent through Wulfaet Boetman, the captain of a ship trading between Nieuwport, Belgium and Great Yarmouth, who seems to have provided a vital link between the refugees in Norwich and their families in the Low Countries.

Leonard Keerlinck to his brother-in-law Victor de Vinck, 31 August 1567. 'Bad times are at hand for Flanders; more can be had at Norwich for a penny than for three in Ypres'. If Victor is planning to come to England, he is advised to 'make haste to come before winter and do not bring more than is necessary to keep house, for the freight is dear'.

Clement Baet to his wife, 5 September 1567. He arrived in Norwich on 3 September, and met many friends, 'who rejoiced much at his coming'. He tells his wife to sell what she has and come over: 'there is good trade in bays and I will look out for a house as quickly as I can to get into business, for then it will be easy to make money. I will get ready the gear for making the bays against your coming. Bring all your and your daughter's clothing for people go well clad here. Go to Nieuwport, the women will help you well. Let your sister know that Lien's trade is no use, for they only work at

The invitation to the first thirty 'Strangers', from 1566.

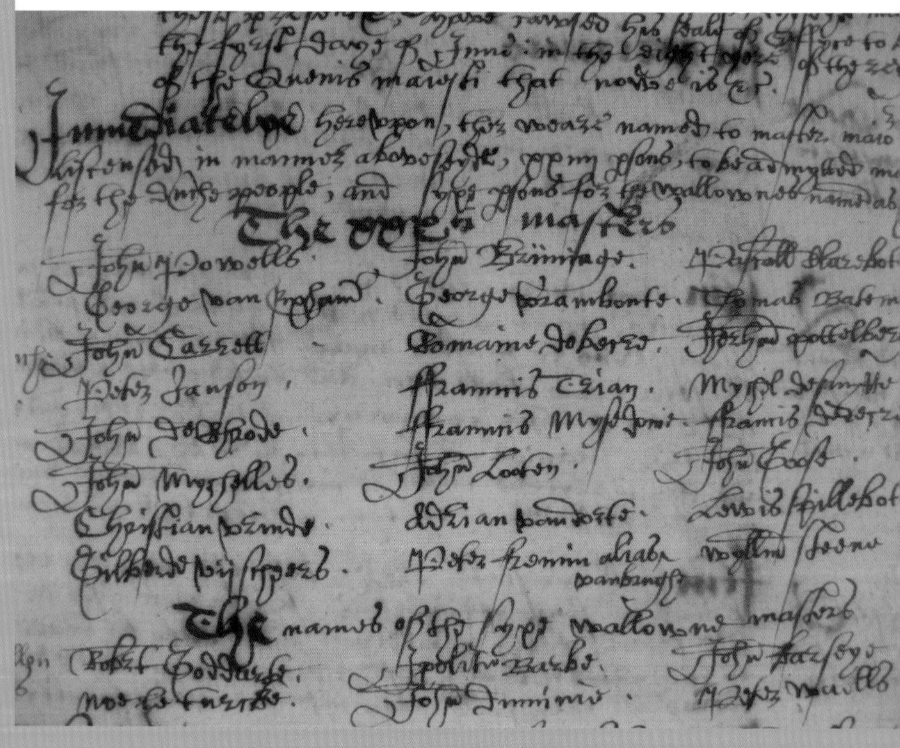

bay work here… I let you know that we are merry and happy with each other. May God give you the same loving peace and riches as we have here at Norwich. It is very dear to hear the word of God peacefully'.

Most letters are from men, but a few are from women. Mayekin (surname unknown) wrote back to her parents, Pieter de Wert and his wife, in 1567 saying that she and her husband had been asked to come over to Norwich because the expense of the journey could easily be made up there, and because God's service was free there. The couple were taking up a new profession: 'we both learn bay-weaving'. On 3 October 1567, the unnamed wife of Jacques Rollier wrote to her son Tarkin telling him to send over all the unfinished caps they had left behind. She had a good voyage, arriving in Norwich in good health on 29 September. On the following day she wrote to a friend, Inghele Nechebaent, asking her to tell all their neighbours that she and Jacques had enjoyed a good passage across, 'with many others', and were both well: they were living near the Market, by the church.

Another letter was written two years later, by Gilles Navegeer to his grandmother, 13 September 1569. He states that his father, mother and sisters are well. 'We have been at Norwich a little less than two years, where we are living in great quietness and peace and the word of God is preached much among us'. He understands the fatherland to be in great trouble and uproar. For more than six months he learned bookbinding, but that gave too little profit, so in 1569 he has taken to another trade, by which he hopes to do better. His eldest sister, Maeyken, is with Pieter Bake of Ypres, who has a brewery at Norwich where she works. His brother, Willekin, is learning the trade of a cutler; his father works in a thread twist factory; his mother does outwork; another sister, little Maeyken, spins thread; Synken, presumably an infant, 'plays all day'. He mentions that 'Gaige' had died in the fourth week after Whit Sunday: we do not know who Gaige was.

Such letters between refugees and their families bring to life their daily concern: any such correspondence by more recent immigrant groups should be carefully preserved, they will make an important record for future generations.

DUTCH AND FRENCH IMMIGRANTS

The immigrant community, swollen far beyond the original 300 by these many refugees fleeing from persecution, came to form a large part of the city: it is a reasonable guess that one third of the population of Norwich in the 1570s and 1580s was made up of Dutch and French speaking immigrants new to the city. It is impossible to know exactly what proportion of the total population they made, although the number of immigrants is well recorded as the authorities made a count of them on several occasions. The paradox is that no census was ever made of the English, so we simply do not know what the total population of the city at this date was!

By 1568, according to a return of 'aliens' in the city archives, there were 1,132 Dutch speakers and 339 French speakers in the city. In November 1569 the number of Strangers was calculated, in a return for the Privy Council, at 2,591 (752 men, 681 women, 26 servants, 1132 children).

The figures included a number of sailors who had recently been shipwrecked, showing that the crossing was not without its risks. In October 1571 the total number of Strangers was 4,013 (1,056 men, 1,095 women, 1,862 children). Another calculation of the same date produced the figure 3,925 (868 men of the Dutch nation, 203 men of the Walloon nation, 1,173 women of both nations, 1,681 children under the age of fourteen, of whom 666 were born in England). The city calculated that 355 people had arrived since 25 March 1571, made up of 85 Dutchmen, 25 Walloon men, 85 women and an unspecified number of children – and also one Frenchman from Dieppe.

The figures can be broken down into wards: the two wards with over 500 immigrants were West Wymer with 827 and Mid Wymer with 577. The wards over the water also had high numbers – 471 in Colegate, 412 in Coslany and 462 in Fyebridge. There were fewer immigrants in the other wards, 208 in Ber Street for example. Only one ward had less than 100 newcomers – St Giles, with just 62.

It is a reasonable guess that by 1579 there might have been as many as 6,000 immigrants in the city, most living in the St. Benedict's Street/ Hungate area or north of the river. Then disaster struck the community.

1579 PLAGUE

Norwich, like all cities, was subject to waves of plague and the one in 1579 was exceptionally severe: between June 1579 and February 1580, almost five thousand people in the city died from plague, according to weekly figures kept by the city authorities. From October onwards they distinguish in the figures between English people and 'Strangers'. The outbreak was passed its peak by then, but out of the 830 people dying of plague in the next few months, at least 600 were Strangers. If the same proportion applied during the summer then the total number of Strangers dying of the plague in 1579 would have been at least 2,500 and perhaps more. It is not clear why such a high proportion of immigrants died. Did they live in especially poor and over-crowded conditions? Had they not yet built up sufficient immunity to the local strain of the disease? Both factors probably played their part. Some of the Strangers were buried in local parish churches. Burials in St Michael at Plea include several immigrants, such as the family of William Bartringham, 'the painter, Dutchman'. His daughter Judith was buried on 7 August, his son David on 26 August, William himself on 30 August, and Esther, another daughter, on 24 September. This example shows the devastating effect that plague could have on an immigrant family.

In 1583, after almost two decades of immigration from the Low Countries, and after the devastation caused by the 1579 plague, the authorities wanted once more to know how many Strangers were living in the city. The figures were:

Male Strangers	*1,128*
Female Strangers	*1,358*
Children born abroad	*815*
Children born in England	*1,376*
Total number of Strangers	***4,677***

There had been no apparent increase since 1571, and the large number of children born in this country shows that many of the newcomers had been in England a considerable time. However, given the number of deaths by plague, there must have been a large number of new immigrants to maintain the figure at about the same level as in the years before the plague.

The new immigrants of the 1560s to 1580s largely merged into the local community remarkably quickly, within two generations. A note in the city archives records that the number of persons in the Dutch congregation was 1,200 in 1613, falling to 999 in 1624 and to 678 in 1634 – of whom 575 were second generation immigrants, that is born in Norwich to immigrant parents. Many of the others may have returned to the Continent, but most will have ceased to be regarded as part of the Dutch congregation because they had been assimilated into the city's population, attending Anglican churches.

SHARING SKILLS

The majority of the incomers were weavers, men like Jan de Turk and Guy de Lewalle. Turk was a wool comber from Flanders. He arrived in Norwich in 1567 with three children and a pregnant wife, who soon gave birth to their fourth child. Lewalle was a Walloon who entered into a contract to serve some Norwich business men in the making of bays in 1576. A 1573 dispute between two immigrant Dutchmen, Thomas Hodgeson and Thomas Bateman, concerning linen cloth is significant in that all the witnesses, themselves Dutch, agreed that there had been an agreement between the two – which had been written in Dutch. Members of the immigrant community were – naturally – using their own language in which to conduct their business, in the process creating records that were unintelligible to the authorities.

The 'new draperies' that the Strangers brought were originally characterised very simply: Dutch drapery was 'wet and greasy', that of the Walloons 'dry and coloured'. Such definitions became too simple as new fabrics were developed. The two new communities could be rivals: in November 1575, the elders of the Dutch community came to the mayor's court with a new material, 'bombazine'. They asked that they should have a monopoly of its production: the Walloons complained that this was unfair on them. The Dutch satisfied the court that they had been the first to produce bombazine and they were allowed their monopoly. In 1577, the Walloons themselves went to the court, asking for new regulations for the making of 'mockadoes', and that the Dutch be ordered to observe these new rules.

As this suggests, the incomers were very inventive at producing new products, or at least promoting a new product, perhaps only a very little different to a previous one but marketed under an exciting new name. Fuller wrote about Norwich stuffs in the 1650s, 'A pretty pleasing name, complying with the buyer's fancy, much befriendeth a stuff in the sale thereof': the pleasure in buying some new fashion or style, simply because it is new, was as great in the 16th and 17th centuries as it is today and the immigrants were at least as quick as the other traders to take advantage of this side of human nature.

The skills that these immigrants brought were passed on to English workers: in 1576, for example, Richard Whittrell, a Norfolk tailor deposed in the mayor's court that he was happy for his 16-year old son Robert to become an apprentice to Charles Droghbroot to learn the art of bay-weaving. Related skills also developed among the immigrants, and these new skills were learned by English apprentices. Peter de Keyser acquired a letter of denization in 1584 and became a freeman in 1587 as a hosier. He became constable of St Peter Mancroft ward in 1592, the first of the incomers known to have achieved an official position in the city. Between 1613 and 1619, 17 out of 29 people registering as hosiers were of Dutch or Walloon descent.

Dyeing and dyes were an important part of the skills that the immigrants brought. Cornelis de Ram 'tabellarius' [courier] had come from Zeeland in 1567 with his wife and two children. A legal case in which he was involved in 1573 revealed details of the industry: it was said that two years earlier he had carried 'coccesnell' from London. This was the dye stuff cochineal and it was not a large quantity: he carried it attached to his saddle in a blue purse. The witness, John de Horne, remembered the occasion as he had to help Ram up onto his horse for the journey to Norwich – either Ram was ill when he set out on his hundred-mile journey or he was conforming to the stereotype that the English had of the Dutch – their drunkenness!
In 1590, Gyles Cambye, an immigrant dyer told the mayor's court that he was trading with Arthur Rotye, another immigrant now living in London, in goods dyed in green, in which skill Rotye was an expert: could he be induced to come to Norwich and teach his skills to others? He could, and he taught his art to an English dyer named William Morley and his apprentices.

Pin-making was another skill the incomers were happy to pass on. Whittrell's younger son, Eustace, became apprentice to Nicholas Vanbuston, pinner, while in 1581

The Great Hospital – where pin-making was taught by Nicholas Beoscom in 1581.

the Great Hospital appointed Nicholas Beoscom, to teach his skills in pin-making to the children there. Both men were recent immigrants to the city.

The immigrant community provided opportunities for English girls too, such as 14-year-old Susan Browne and her unnamed sister, orphans, each of whom was found a job in service with a Dutchman, Robert Cook and John Crolond, respectively.

MERCHANTS

Other incomers were traders or merchants rather than manufacturers. The sale of goods from one foreigner to another was always looked on with suspicion. In 1600, a Walloon wool comber with the very English name of John Lee found himself placed in Norwich Castle by the Admiralty bailiff – his crime was buying meat and carrying yarn and conveying it over the sea. Another incomer with an English-sounding name was John Williamson, who bought and sold wool to and from foreigners.

One immigrant, Jacques de Hem, became a prominent city merchant: in 1595 he was chosen by the city to buy up rye from Amsterdam for the city's grain reserves, and to transport it back to the city. Six years later he was in trouble for selling four bales of madder to another immigrant, Giles Carmby: the transaction did not take place in the Madder Market as might be expected, but in the parish of St Peter Mancroft, presumably in the Market Place. Jacques became a freeman in 1602, paying the enormous sum of £50: he must have been a very wealthy man, but his life had its tragedies. His wife Anna died in October 1603 giving birth to their tenth child, who also died. The ten children, five boys and five girls, can still just be seen on Anna's memorial in the church of Saint Michael at Plea. Jacques later married again, to Sarah Derick the daughter of Abraham Derick and they had several more children, one of whom, Judith, was baptised in the Dutch Church in 1618, although the local parish church was the baptism place of choice for most of the others. Jacques himself died in May 1624, aged 76, soon followed by the most well-known of his sons, Tobias, also a very wealthy Norwich merchant, who died in July 1629 aged 41. All are buried in

St Michael at Plea. Tobias bequeathed to the city the silver cup known as the De Hem flagon. He had had a son, also named Tobias, baptised in the Dutch Church in 1619: the mother, Susanne, is described as 'syner huisvrouwe', housekeeper rather than wife to this merchant and second generation immigrant.

The case of Tannekyn de Boys, before the Norwich authorities in 1573, shows how strong trading links were across the sea. Her husband, Domynyk had recently died and the issue was whether she had received the money due to her from his business interests. He had been in partnership with another 'Stranger', Laurence Pytt, dealing primarily in salt. Another business associate was Jan van Vive of Norwich, and the two sums in dispute were allegedly in his hands: about £20 for an assignment of salt, and also the sum of sixteen 'angels' that he had been paid to look after the de Boys' children and provide them with clothing. As a further complication, another £7 of money due for the purchase or sale of salt was in the hands of yet another associate, Francis Clarke, who was in Flanders.

Both the de Boys were in the habit of travelling to and fro across the North Sea (which is presumably why their children needed looking after): Tannekyn had taken one angel from van Vive on the occasion of 'her going into Flanders', while her husband had accommodation in Zeeland. This ease of travel is further illustrated in that one witness, Adrian Basten, was actually in Zeeland when he received a letter from Norwich about the case: he journeyed to the house where de Boys lived to try and ascertain the facts from his landlady there. The case led to an unseemly shouting match before the Dutch congregation in Norwich, but it is not known how it turned out. There must have been many contacts between Norwich and Europe through the medium of the incomers, but they tend to show up only when disputes led to court cases. In 1588, merchants in Norwich were exporting bays to Hamburg Fair, while five years later Mallyard Rickwarde, a stranger merchant living in Norwich, bought

Memorial to Anna de Hem, St Michael at Plea.

'silk Cyprus' in Rotterdam. In both cases disagreements about price and quality led to complaints, but no doubt there were many hundreds of similar instances that were profitable to all the parties involved.

If international trade was regulated by the authorities, so was localised shopping. The first group of immigrants was not intended to include traders such as bakers, shoemakers and brewers, but many soon came over among the refugees. The city authorities tried to prevent immigrants selling to people in the city apart from members of their own community. In 1573 the city authorities ordered the bakers within the community not to buy corn on the Market before 1pm, and forbade them to bake any white bread, cakes, custards 'or any such dainties' to sell. The frequency with which such orders were issued suggests that they were being flouted: no doubt people were tempted to try new styles of food and other produce.

In 1599, a Frenchman named Marshall Dede was before the court for buying 60 pints of butter on the market – 20 pints were ordered to be resold by the Sergeant of the Market at three pence a pint, and it was decided that Strangers should in future only buy enough butter to feed their family for a week. Not all butter was for human consumption – whey butter was used to grease a fleece before spinning: in fact it was forbidden to use 'any oil or other filthy stuff'. Butter and related goods were part of a weaver's stock-in-trade: when an immigrant named Jacob Le Poultre died, his property in his house in St George Colegate included fifteen old butter barrels and twenty pounds of whey butter along with his loom and wool combs.

PRINTING

The refugees brought many other skills to the city, including printing: the first printer in Norwich was Anthony de Solempne, who came to England from Brabant in 1567, with his wife and two sons. The first book ever printed in the city was Solempne's *Belijdenisse Ende* or *Confession of Faith*, published in 1567. In the next four years he printed eight books in the city, all except one in Dutch – showing that there were plenty of Dutch people in the city, refugees and others, who were capable of reading, and who wanted books in their own language: the will of one refugee, Joos de Ram, who

Anthony de Solempne blue plaque – the first printer in Norwich.

died in 1577 specifically mentions his 'bookes as well lattyn as Dutch'. Some of the books Solempne printed are in the Norfolk and Norwich Millennium Library. He became a freeman of Norwich in 1570 and took on the selling of wine from the Rhineland, apparently giving up printing. Two further Dutch books printed in Norwich were probably by another refugee printer, Albert Christian from Holland. Booksellers included Cornelius van Hille, coming from Flanders with his wife and son, and Peter Jass, from Zeeland who brought his wife, his son and a female servant. All arrived in 1567.

MEDICINE

There were several doctors of medicine among the incomers, such as Matthew Richius, who arrived in Norwich from Flanders in 1567. He died in 1593 and is buried in St George Tombland.

Another Dutch physician was Martin van Kurnebeck who died in 1578, followed by his wife the following year: their tomb can still be seen in the church of St Mary Coslany. Flemish-born Kurnebeck was a well-travelled man, having obtained his degree in Bologna, Italy. He became physician to both the Duke of Norfolk and the Bishop of Norwich, John Parkhurst. Parkhurst once wrote that, when he suffered from fever and pain from his bladder stone, he was looked after by 'three physicians, deeply attached to me, one English, one Flemish, the third Hungarian. Through their efforts, but by the power of God Almighty I recovered'. Another family of doctors was that of the Cropps. John Cropp was an immigrant from Flanders, while his son, also named John Cropp, was born in 1572, possibly in Norwich. The latter is mentioned in a letter of Katherine Paston after a neighbour of hers had hurt his arm: 'on Monday, Mr Crope I think will take it in hand, first by physic and after by applying strengthy things to it'. The 1622 return of 'aliens' mentions one surgeon, the aforementioned John Cropp, a physician, Abraham Hacker, and a barber surgeon, Peter Hiborne.

GOLDSMITHS

As we have seen, there were several immigrant goldsmiths in the city and the crisis in the Low Countries brought more. George Fenne, a Dutch immigrant (his father was born in Utrecht), purchased the freedom in 1567: in the following year he was fined for a minor offence under the name of 'Dutch George'. He was an important figure both in the Dutch Church and in the world of the goldsmith. He died in 1587. The well-known goldsmith Peter Peterson was born in the city but was of immigrant descent: he made four silver communion cups for the Dutch Church in about 1580. Among the many possessions listed in his will was 'my chest of Flanders make', perhaps a family heirloom.

CLOCK-MAKING

Another skill brought by the Strangers was that of clock and watch-making. There had been clock-makers in the city in earlier times, such as Walter Orloger, freeman of the city in 1420, who made a new clock for Norwich Cathedral. At least three families of Strangers had this skill. Jacques van Barton, freeman in 1605, may have been the son of Jacob Bertin, a smith, who came to Norwich from Brabant in 1567 with his wife and five children. His son James followed him into the profession, becoming a clock-maker in 1629. Ahasuerus Fromanteel was the son of Murdoch Fromanteel an immigrant chair maker. In 1631, he married Maria de Bruijne, who came from a community of immigrants in Colchester: they had seven children, all baptised in the Dutch Church in Norwich. His sister Elizabeth married Andries Priem in 1646. Priem himself had been born in Norwich in 1619, the son of Dutch-immigrant parents, Andries and Susanna. He spent most of his life in London, working as a clock-maker under the name Andrew Prime. In 1675, he and his son Abraham – 'experts in clock work' – were asked to repair the clock on St Andrew's Hall 'being of great use to that part of the city, but now being in great decay': the cost was not to exceed £15, of which the Dutch congregation would pay £5. Priem returned to Norwich in about 1682 and died in St Andrew's parish in 1710.

POTTERY

Many other occupations were represented among the new inhabitants of the city. Three early immigrants, coming over in 1567, were Jasper and Joris Andries and Jacob Jansen, potters who specialised in maiolica ware – tin-glazed earthenware pottery used in making paving tiles and for jars in pharmacies. The Andries were brothers, sons of Guido Andries, an Italian said to have introduced the art of tin-glazed earthenware to Antwerp in about 1510. Jansen was from Amsterdam and soon moved on to London. In a petition to the Queen they claimed that they were the first to introduce and to exercise 'the potters' science' in Britain. John Carsey was a brewer as well as a merchant: when he took up his freedom in 1570, he paid the very large sum of £100 as a bond not to buy or sell any merchandise not connected with brewing. In 1586, the authorities of St Peter Mancroft paid Abraham Panvoorth seven shillings for new glass and mending other pieces of glass in the church.

Some immigrants thought it worthwhile to have the fact that their children were born in England registered in the mayor's court. The formal record is in Latin, and the phrase used for the Dutch Church is 'ecclesia Belgicae'. In 1601, John Cruso recorded the births of his children John (born 1592), Timothy (1594), Aquila (1597) and Maria (1599); the two oldest children were born in St George Colegate parish, the two youngest in St Saviour's parish.

Flemish weavers' tapestry in St Peter Mancroft. This section shows Jesus (standing) as a gardener, dressed as the many Dutch gardeners among the Strangers would have been.

John Cruso, the father, was a cloth merchant: he and his wife Jane Verlincke were refugees from Flanders. John, the son, became a musketeer and later captain of the Dutch militia in the city. He is not known to have had any other military experience, yet he became the first man to write a book on cavalry strategy in England. His book, *Militarie Instructions for the Cavalrie*, was published in 1632. His books were heavily dependent upon books describing Dutch wars. John and his wife Rebecca had at least two children born in Norwich and baptised in the Dutch Church: Ann in 1617 and John in 1618. John junior went on to study at Cambridge University in 1632.

GARDENING

Another characteristic of the new Dutch residents of Norwich was their love of gardening, especially flowers: they introduced the tulip to England. Joos Brake, gardener and seller of herbs, was one of the earliest immigrants, coming over from Zeeland with his wife and son in 1567.
As early as 1575, the Dutch in the city were seen as gardening experts: Sir Thomas Kytson of Hengrave Hall in Suffolk summoned a Dutchman from the city, whose name is not known, to advise him on landscaping the Hall garden. He was paid forty shillings for 'clipping the knots, altering the alleys, setting the ground, finding herbs, and bordering the same'. In the 1624 subsidy rolls for the city, the immigrant paying the most tax was Malliard Widoote of Carrow, 'husbandman and gardener'.

Thomas Fuller wrote of the city in the 17th century: 'Norwich is (as you please) either a City in an Orchard,

Opposite: Strangers' weaving work: tapestry in St Peter Mancroft church made by Flemish weavers, 1573.

or an Orchard in a City, so equally are Houses and Trees blended in it'. Fuller was full of praise for the Dutch, who 'brought hither with them, not only their profitable crafts, but pleasurable curiosities. They were the first who advanced the use and reputation of Flowers in this City'. In the early 17th century, Florists' Feasts were being held in the city, attended by both Dutch and English – the Chelsea Flower Festivals of their day. In a 1622 list of incomers, no less than nine were described as gardeners, including William and Peter Rottengoose, Tobias Barton and Christian Vervinke.

Cases of 'scrumping' also indicate the contribution of the immigrant community. In 1582, three Norwich men – probably little more than boys, one was a servant or apprentice – were whipped for breaking into the orchard of Gyles Vanderbrook, alien, and carrying off apples and pears. In 1590, five young Norwich men were charged with illegally entering a close sown with roots outside St Stephen's Gates, the property of Mr Vertngose. There is a tapestry in St Peter Mancroft church, woven by Flemish weavers in 1573, perhaps as an altar frontal – the image it portrays of Jesus as a gardener, with hat and spade, reminds us of the importance of gardening within the Dutch community.

THE 'POLITIC MEN' AND POVERTY

The Strangers were regulated by a group of men chosen from among themselves and known as the 'politic men'. They had to deal with the problem of poverty within the community. A few of the incomers were wealthy, such as Martin van Kurenbeck, who was the only Stranger paying the tax known as landgable in 1568-70. Presumably other immigrants were not landowners – yet – and certainly some were very poor – the 1568 return says that 'four or five couples dwelt together in one family'. Most will have rented rather than owned their houses, like the immigrants who rented parts of the Bridewell building from the city authorities – their rents varied from sixty shillings a year paid by Peter Debryne for four chambers, down to the single room rented by John Cordyner for eighteen shillings a year. The authorities could intervene if they suspected exploitation. In 1586, there was a dispute between an English widow, Margaret Elwyn, and a young immigrant girl who lived in her house, Katheryn Verbeck: the court decided that Katheryn should pay three pence a week for her rent and could keep the rest of her earnings.

On Queen Elizabeth's visit to Norwich in 1578, the Strangers gave her a silver gilt cup. She gave £30 to relieve the poor – £19 to the Dutch, £11 to the Walloons. The money was passed to Thomas Layer who gave it to the deacons of the communities: Anthony de Solempne and Zegor Wittewronghele of the Dutch congregation and John Debraban and Thomas Delatombe for the Walloons. This was done in the presence of the Dutch minister Harmanus Modert and the Walloon minister Leodwycus Maupin. As this suggests, the immigrant communities looked after their own poor. In times of crisis, this could be a problem; in 1587, after a decline in trade, the Dutch said they could not do so and the city gave them £10 it had received from taxes on their cloths. Two years later, the Walloons made the same complaint: the city gave them £10 out of its treasury and two local preachers collected no less than £28 from 'well affected' people.

One task of the politic men was to assign guardians or tutors to orphaned children within the communities: in days of high mortality it was far more common for children to become orphans than it is today. One man who played a full part in this social-care aspect of Norwich immigrant life was Noah le Turcke, a weaver from Flanders who was one of the first arrivals with his wife: all their children were born in Norwich. He acted as 'guarantor' for one orphan Marie Bronnest and as a guardian to another, Jan Callet. Noah himself died in 1587, leaving three orphaned children – Noah, Elizabeth and Samuel – for whom tutors were appointed. Hendrick Gheerat also frequently acted as one of the politic men assigning guardians to orphans but his family too saw the system from the other side: he must have died before March 1586 when his five orphaned children – Gerson, Eleasar, Susanne, Hendrick and Abigail – were themselves assigned guardians. Jacques de Hem was also part of this support system, becoming one of the guardians to the five Crekells children – a boy and four little girls – orphaned in 1590 on the death of their father Victor. Other family tragedies included the five de Corte children orphaned in 1583, and the five children of Pierre Marchant, who became orphans when their father died in 1584: other members of the immigrant community were appointed as their carers.

We know the fate of only a very few of these orphans, those girls (and they are only a small minority of the orphan girls) whose marriage is recorded. Some were already almost of marriageable age, like Judith Barbien, who was given two guardians on 15 June 1585, on the death of her father, Jan. Less than four months later she ceased to be the responsibility of the politic men, as she married Pierre Hubert. However, Lydia Mouesnoet, who became orphaned on the death of her father Rainier in 1586, is only recorded as marrying Abraham van Wegge over thirteen years later, in November 1599: one of her two guardians was Francis Trioen, who, like le Turcke, was one of the original thirty masters.

COMMUNITY CHURCHES

Each community had its own church. The Bishop of Norwich, John Parkhurst had himself been a refugee because of his religion, living in exile in Zurich during the reign of Queen Mary. He allowed the French-speaking community to worship in his own chapel in the grounds of the Bishop's Palace. There were over 90 children baptised here in the French Church in

Rembrandt

one year alone, 1600. When a later bishop reclaimed it in the 1630s, the community worshipped instead in the old church of St Mary the Less, which they had previously been using as a hall for marking their goods. Services continued here for two centuries, coming to an end in 1832.

The French community had several distinguished pastors. Pierre de Laune was born in 1574, the son of a Huguenot divine and physician. He became pastor of the Norwich French Church in 1599. He translated the Anglican Book of Common Prayer into French and presented the City Library with a copy of this work in 1614. In December 1655, Isaac Clement was appointed his coadjutor. Clement was born at Middleburg in 1632 and had been appointed minister of the French Church in Norwich in 1650, aged only eighteen. He went back to Holland on leave of absence in 1657 and wrote from there to the Church saying that his parents did not want him to return: he died at Flushing in 1666, in his early thirties. He was succeeded by Jacques le Franc who himself resigned in 1664, becoming Anglican rector of St Clement's four years later. Le Franc was a friend of the diarist John Evelyn, and a very scholarly figure: he wrote at least one theological work and is supposed to have discussed original sin with the theologian Jeremy Taylor. There was no language difficulty between the Englishman and the immigrant: their discussion was carried on in Latin!

The Dutch community worshipped in Blackfriars' Hall. The most well-known of the pastors there was Johannes or John Elison, who, along with his wife Maria, had the distinction of being painted by Rembrandt, the only English residents to have their portraits painted by the Dutch Master. The portraits are now in the Museum of Fine Arts in Boston, U.S.A. Elison was born in the Low Countries in about 1581 and went to Leiden University, becoming pastor at Norwich in about 1604. On his death, he was succeeded as pastor by his Norwich-born son Theophilus, who had been educated at Cambridge: he served for forty years, dying in 1679. There are plaques to both on the wall of the Hall: in an early example of a multilingual text, that to the father is in three languages – Dutch, English and Latin. Another of John's sons, John the younger, was a wealthy merchant in Amsterdam: he probably commissioned the Rembrandt portraits of his parents when they visited him in Amsterdam in 1633-4.

However, the numbers worshipping in these churches soon became comparatively small, as most strangers integrated into the community. Peter Peterson asks in his will to be buried in the church of St Andrew 'in the chapel where I usually sit': he must have worshipped there for many years. Memorials to Dutch-speaking incomers in the city's Anglican churches include those to van Kurnebeck, who died in 1579, in St Mary Coslany, and the de Hem family, in St Michael at Plea.

Opposite: Rembrandt painting of Maria Elison, 1634.
Photograph © June 2012 Museum of Fine Arts, Boston.

The French Church did try to keep hold of three people in the 1620s who wanted to withdraw from the church and worship with local Anglican groups. The three – Denis Lermyte, John Desormeaux and Samuel Camby – were all very wealthy, which is why the church wanted to hang onto them: no doubt many less financially significant people were making a similar move at the time without fuss. The merging of the French-speaking and English communities can also be illustrated from the career of Peter de Laune. He was installed rector of Harleston and Redenhall in 1629, while retaining his pastorship of the French Church. The two communities were no longer mutually exclusive: one could be part of, and contribute to, both. The tradition of holding occasional services in the immigrants' home language continued into the 19th century in the French Church and well into the 20th century in the Dutch Church. It was not many years before regime change in their home countries meant that the refugees from the Low Countries could return home, and some did so, while others had settlements or business interests on both sides of the North Sea. Some of the Dutch cities took active steps to encourage the immigrants to return. In 1577, for example the city of Leiden sent a delegation to Norwich, led by Jan Teutons and Lodewijk de Rijckes, and some did make the journey, where they registered as citizens.

Another Leiden-born Protestant, Jan Paedts had been a refugee to Norwich in 1568. He went back to Leiden a few years later, and in 1577 he returned to Norwich to ask Carolus Rijckwaant (alias Theophilus) to come back to Leiden to preach. In 1590, two Flemish drapers in Norwich, Adriaan Tarte and Joos de Heedere, were asked by the Leiden authorities to return there and work in the city. However, a very great number of the refugees clearly felt they had settled in Norwich and stayed in the city.

THE CANARIES

The Dutch community brought into Norwich several benefits that are now taken for granted as part of city life. The most notable is the canary, brought by them as pets. They soon caught on in the city, which became well known for its canary breeding, even producing its own particular breed, the Norwich plain head. The canary has become the symbol of the city, and breeding and showing birds has been a Norwich speciality for centuries. In time, the original introduction of the birds into Norwich by the Dutch became forgotten and the canary became a symbol for the city. Local newspapers in the following centuries are full of descriptions of shows. To take a random example, in just one fortnight in 1893, there were competitions at the *Kings' Arms* in St Martin's, the *Mariners* in Mariners' Lane and the *Rose* in St Augustine's, and two all-day shows were held on the same day at the *Shuttles*, Heigham Street and the *Sons of Commerce* in Thorn Lane. Each event might involve up to three hundred birds and people travelled from as far away as London for them. The event at the

Left: A Norwich citizen with his pet canaries – a symbol of Norwich.
Above: Dutch gables in Cathedral Close.

Shuttles centred upon a bird exhibited by J Burrell, his 'Living Wonder', a pure Norwich crest. Like a boxer, he challenged anyone to match it, and when the judges did indeed decide a rival bird was superior, the local press devoted as long an article to the decision as it would to a disputed boxing contest. In 1908, Norwich women marched from Liverpool Street station to Hyde Park in support of a major suffragette meeting being held there: the Eastern Daily Press reporter noted that, when the Norwich banners passed by on the way to Hyde Park, the London crowd called out 'Canaries'. He was not sure if this referred to the local football team or whether it was 'a playful way of expressing the truly Cockney idea that Norwich people all live by breeding little birds'. In the 1912 floods in the city, one of the saddest sights was to see drowned canaries, trapped in their cages, being carried along in the water. This enthusiasm for the birds still continues: the Dalai Lama bought canaries from local fancier (and ex-Canary, that is, footballer!) Chris Goodall in the 1970s. The green and yellow colours and the name Canaries adopted by Norwich City Football Club are a direct descendant of the bird- and flower- loving immigrants who arrived in the city more than four centuries ago.

GABLES

The Dutch also brought new building forms, still to be seen in the city. Many local buildings have the rounded gable, known as the Dutch gable and reminiscent of towns in Holland. They also brought in the pantile, a form of tile in the shape of an 'S', common in the East of England but rarely found elsewhere. Look out for these in the city – they often have a black glaze. Crow-stepped gables, a characteristic of Flemish buildings, also began to appear in Norfolk.

CHAPTER 5

French Refugees from Religious Persecution

The French Church was founded by French-speaking refugees from the Low Countries. There were also several waves of refugees from religious persecution from France itself over the centuries, some of whose families have added greatly to Norwich cultural and intellectual life.

Opposite: The writer Harriet Martineau, descendent of Gaston Martineau who fled France in the late 17th century.

One example of a French refugee family is that of Ninham. Henry Ninham was a member of the Norwich School of Art, who painted very English pictures of Norwich, mainly of its buildings. He was from a refugee family: his ancestor had fled from a horrifying sequence of events, the Saint Bartholomew's Day Massacre. This mass-murder of French Protestants began in Paris on 24 August 1572. Their leader Admiral Coligny was the first victim; his death was followed by the killing of minor leaders and of all Protestants within reach of the soldiers, and of the mob who joined in the chance to exterminate their sworn enemies. The massacre continued even after a royal order to stop, and it spread from Paris into other sections of France. An estimated 3,000 were killed in Paris, 70,000 in all of France. Naturally, many surviving Protestants fled and some, like Ninham's ancestor, came to England. Thus this very English painter is another example of contribution made to the culture of the city by a descendant of refugees.

THE HUGUENOTS

The Edict of Nantes in 1598 established religious toleration in France. This was gradually whittled away in the later years of the 17th century. The Edict was finally revoked in 1685, and a large number of Protestant French people had to flee the country. These are the people who are known as Huguenots, and they have made a major contribution to Norwich life. The older community of French-speakers from the Low Countries were strengthened by these incomers, and it is not always easy to distinguish between them, especially as changing boundaries have brought parts of what were considered as the Low Countries into the country we now call France.

Many of the Huguenots were associated with weaving, especially silk. W G Sebald, an immigrant himself, whose story is told in a later chapter, wrote about the great contribution these immigrant silk weavers made to the city: 'By 1750, a bare two generations later, the Huguenot master weavers of Norwich had risen to become the wealthiest, most influential and cultivated class of entrepreneurs in the entire kingdom. In their factories and those of their suppliers there was the greatest imaginable commotion, day in, day out, and it is said in a history of silk manufacture in England, that a traveller approaching Norwich under the black sky of a winter night would be amazed by the glare over the city, caused by light coming from the windows of the workshops, still busy at this late hour'. This contribution to city life is commemorated in the mulberry tree planted behind the French Church.

THE COLOMBINES AND THE MARTINEAUS

The Huguenots included two families who became well-known in Norwich, the Colombines and the Martineaus. Francois Jacolumbine fled to Norwich from France in about 1698 and practised 'physic' [medicine] in the city. His son Peter Colombine, born in 1697, married Marie Martineau in 1719. Peter became a freeman, as a worsted weaver, in 1720, was an alderman from 1752 and served as mayor in 1755, showing how quickly an immigrant family became part of the city establishment. His son, Francis, also became mayor of Norwich but later fell on hard times, resigning his aldermancy in 1802: the city came to the rescue of this second-generation immigrant, granting him and his daughter an annuity of £100 because of the family's financial problems.

The first of the Martineau family to come to the city was Gaston, a physician. The family supplied several generations of medical men, as well as merchants and writers. The best-known, Harriet Martineau, born in 1802, campaigned against slavery, and was in the forefront of the long path towards equal rights for women: she was one of the four women suffragette leaders Millicent Fawcett regarded as having shown the way forward. Harriet wrote in her autobiography: 'whatever a woman proves herself able to do, society will be thankful to see her do it – just as if she were a man'. She achieved all this despite a life-long struggle with her health, and suffering from deafness.

The Martineau family owned a house and estate outside Norwich, where County Hall and the Norfolk Record Office now stand. The house has been pulled down, but some of the fine trees in the park and the street name of Martineau Lane preserve the memory of this distinguished immigrant family. Further romance in the story lies in the fact that they are direct ancestors of Catherine Middleton, wife of Prince William and future queen of England! Her line of descent can be traced back to Elizabeth Martineau, born in Norwich in 1794, the elder sister of Harriet. Their brother James also played an important part in 19th century Norwich life: he was a prominent writer on religious topics. Harriet Martineau was born in a house in Magdalen Street now marked with a plaque, and James lived in the large Georgian house still to be seen south of the present Anglia Square shopping centre.

Another Huguenot family was that of Rochemont Barbauld, whose grandfather, then aged nine, had been smuggled out of France to Holland in a barrel! Rochemont himself was born in Cassel, Germany, coming to England when he was about 12 years old. He married Anna Aikin in 1774 and for the next 11 years they taught in a school at Palgrave near Diss. The school was funded by Norwich merchants and the pupils included many sons of merchants and professional men in the city. The couple frequently stayed in Norwich, and Rochemont sometimes preached at the Octagon Chapel. They continued to be frequent visitors to the city after they had moved to London in 1787, Rochemont spending two or three months in Norwich on a trial separation from Anna. He died that year, but Anna went on to become one of the most important literary figures of her age, dying in London in 1825.

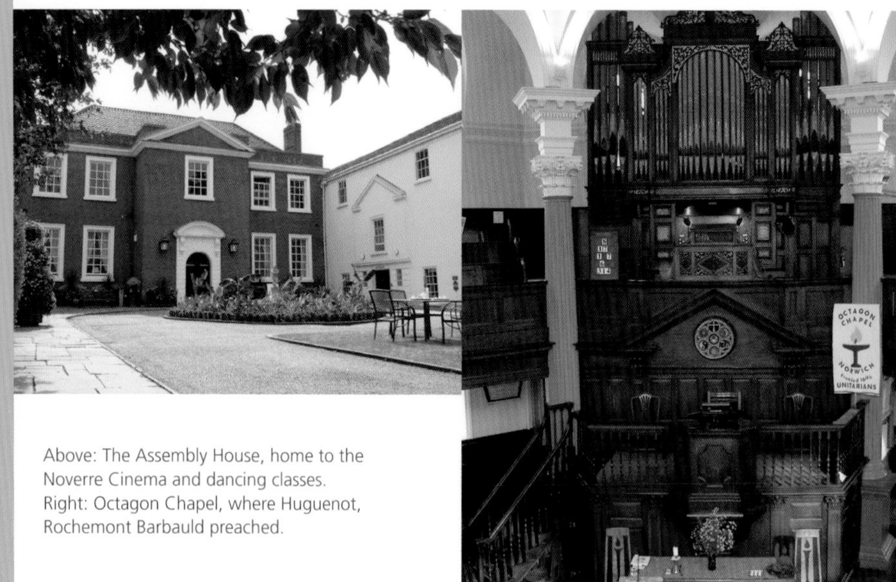

Above: The Assembly House, home to the Noverre Cinema and dancing classes.
Right: Octagon Chapel, where Huguenot, Rochemont Barbauld preached.

Charles Boileau, yet another Huguenot, fled first to Holland, coming to England in 1701. His great grandson, John Peter Boileau, born in 1747 owned Tacolneston Hall, and his son of the same name purchased Ketteringham Hall, later to be home to another group of immigrants, the headquarters of the United States Army Air Force. There is a Boileau Close in Tuckswood: how many of its residents know that the name is that of a refugee family welcomed into England over three centuries ago?

The Assembly House in Norwich includes rooms named after the Noverre family: for many years there was a Noverre Cinema here. The Noverres were dancing masters in Norwich, holding their classes in the Assembly House, and they worshipped at St Stephen's church. They were also an immigrant family, originally from Switzerland, at first living in London: John Georges Noverre, a dancer at the court of King Louis XV in the 1740s, came to England with his brother in 1755. Augustin Noverre retreated to Norwich after injuring a man in an anti-French riot in London, and eventually made it his permanent home, bringing with him his son Francis who became a dancing master in the city. Francis' son, Frank, succeeded his father as dancing master: he taught Norwich a new dance, the polka, after it had been first seen at the Theatre Royal in 1844.

The Revocation of the Edict of Nantes also brought a second group of clock and watch-makers into the city. Thomas Amyot settled in St Peter Mancroft parish. His son, also Thomas was born in 1698, and one of his 'grandfather' (long case) clocks, six feet four inches tall, is in the Bridewell Museum. The third generation of the family produced Peter Amyot, born in 1733, who worked in the Haymarket: one of his clocks is also in the Bridewell. Another clock-maker, Lucas de Caux, arrived in England in about 1693 and worked in London for a decade, moving to Norwich in 1704. He had several children, some baptised in the French Church, others at St Michael at Plea, and was himself buried at the French Church on his death in 1731. Matthew Juler of Norwich was the descendant of a Huguenot refugee who arrived at North Walsham in 1686, while Samuel de Celle, another Huguenot, was working in Norwich in 1710.

Every group of immigrants brings its own characteristics into the cultural mix that makes up Norwich. The Huguenots were responsible for the one new fabric produced in the city at this period – Norwich crape. Crape is a very light, fine material of worsted or mixed worsted and silk, and was fashionable as soon as it was introduced: Daniel Defoe wrote in 1704: 'the first effort of the French refugees was our thin black crape, a manufacture entirely their own, and I refer to the memory of persons conversant in trade, how universally it pleased our people'. They also enriched our language, giving us a new word, and one much used in this book – refugee. Diet also benefits from incomers: the Huguenots are said to have introduced oxtail soup to this country!

The French Church in the city naturally gained many new members at this time. One of the refugees was Pierre Chauvin, minister of Vieillevigne near Nantes who fled to Holland, and was appointed pastor of the Norwich French Church in 1684. The Colombines and the Martineaus were members of the French Church, and plaques in their honour can be seen on its walls. Another man to give it financial support was Thomas Blondell, a woolcomber: in 1730 he bequeathed it a farm in Caister and Stoke Holy Cross, still known as the French Farm. He ordered that his will be read out in the church at a service on 11 January every year, a practice which has long died out of course.

There was a small amount of opposition to the French immigrants at first, promoted by people who claimed that the newcomers were 'Papists', the exact opposite of the truth: as is so often the case, ignorance bred an intolerance based upon fear, which a little common sense would soon blow away.

FRENCH REVOLUTION

A century later, the French Revolution produced a new wave of refugees, principally supporters of the royal family, priests and nuns, and others strongly supportive of Roman Catholicism: members of all these groups found homes in Norwich. One man who became well known in the city was Thomas D'Etreville: a Roman Catholic priest and a teacher at the University of Caen, he fled France in 1792, coming to Norwich in the following year. He lived for a time in Strangers' Hall and taught French and Italian, advertising in local newspapers: his most famous pupil was George Borrow, referred to later. D'Etreville was able to return to his home country after almost 40 years of exile: he died soon after his return to his homeland, in 1843. Another exile was L'Abbe Fleury, who served as priest at Costessey Hall for two years from 1809.

Among those forced out of France at the time of the Revolution were an early group of 'ex-pats', English people who had left England seeking a form of religious lifestyle they were not allowed to practice in this country, the monastic life. One group of nuns ran a

Strangers' Hall, formerly owned by Nicholas Sotherton, the city mayor who welcomed in the Strangers in 1564, has seen many groups of incomers over the centuries. It is now an excellent museum.

school in Paris, where English families who wanted their daughters brought up as Roman Catholics often sent them for their education. This was forcibly closed at the time of the Revolution: the last Reverend Mother and five nuns fled from France and were given sanctuary at Costessey Hall in 1800. Later, a house was found for them in Norwich, in Magdalen Street. Many – but not all – were elderly, and three died there over the next decade, the other three joining other orders. Mary Lloyd (Mother Mary Augustine) died in 1804 aged 89, Margaret Whiteside (Sister Frances Agatha) in 1806, aged only 39, and Elizabeth Green (the last Reverend Mother, Mary Bernard) in 1810, aged 76. All three were buried in the churchyard of St George Colegate, where the burial register simply gives their names and ages: their story as refugees would never have been known if it had not been preserved in other sources. The anonymous author of the first history of the Roman Catholic Church/Cathedral speaks of the French Revolution as a time when 'priests and nuns were scattered abroad like ripe seed blown from some garden in a hurricane', a phrase that could be applied to many of the groups of immigrants into the city over the centuries.

Another refugee from France was Auguste de Bardelin. As a member of the bodyguard of King Louis XVI, he was in great danger of being executed when the Republican regime was established. He fled to England and came to Norwich in about 1792, finding shelter at Crown Point in Trowse, the home of General Money, who had also fought in France. Bardelin supported himself by teaching French and Italian at a Norwich school, and by taking private pupils. Regime change in his home country meant that he was able to return to France in 1814 – after 22 years of exile in Norwich – and he resumed his military career. When he died in 1852, his obituary noted that 'he always referred to his residence at Norwich as the best period of his life': this was a refugee who appreciated the city of his exile.

The French Revolution also indirectly gave us the author of the first-ever book about a vampire – John Polidori. He was born in London in 1795, the son of Gaetano Polidori, an Italian who had lived in Paris until the Revolution led him to move to London in 1790 (the family were Roman Catholics). John Polidori was about twenty years old when he took up medicine in Norwich, and his foreign looks set many a female heart fluttering. Fifteen-year-old Harriet Martineau was one girl who had a crush on him (he was often at her house as he was keen on her older sister, Elizabeth), writing later: 'we younger ones romanced amazingly about him – drew his remarkable profile on the backs of all our letters, dreamed of him, listened to all his marvellous stories, and when he got a concussion of the brain by driving his gig against a tree in Lord Stafford's park (Costessey Hall) were inconsolable'. Polidori's claim to fame came a few years later, after he had left Norwich: he wrote *The Vampyre*, first published in 1819 and the start of an unending stream of novels, later films as well, on the subject.

CHAPTER 6

Immigrants from Black and Ethnic Minorities

There were more black people in Norwich in the 18th and 19th century than is generally supposed. Some were connected with the campaign against slavery – Norwich was one of the places where the anti-slavery movement was strongest – others are known of by pure chance. Three anti-slavery black campaigners with Norwich connections are James Albert Ukawsaw Gronniosaw, Olaudah Equiano and Ignatius Sancho.

Opposite: Cotton – an itinerant tradesman in 1820s Norwich, a painting by John Dempsey.

Gronniosaw (1710-1773) worked for some years in the 1760s as a weaver in the city under the name of James Albert. His origins are explained in his autobiography: 'I was born in the city of Baurnou, my mother was the eldest daughter of the reigning King there. I was the youngest of six children, and particularly loved by my mother, and my grand-father almost doated on me'. Sold into slavery from his native Nigeria, Gronniosaw was granted his freedom in 1748 and soon after entered the British Navy. He married a white weaver, a match disliked by his friends not for racial reasons but for class considerations—according to Gronniosaw, 'because the person [he] had fixed on was poor'. In later life he lived in the West Midlands, and his story was put together and published by 'a young Lady of the town of Leominster, for her own private satisfaction, and without any intention, at first, that it should be made public. But she has now been prevailed on to commit it to the press, both with a view to serve Albert and his distressed family, who have the sole profits arising from the sale of it; and likewise, as it is

Baptisms of freed African slaves, St Peter Mancroft church, 1813.

BAPTISMS solemnized in the Parish of St Peter's Mancroft in the County and City of Norwich in the Year 1813

When Baptised.	Child's Christian Name.	Parent's Name. Christian.	Surname.	Abode.	Quality, Trade, or Profession.	By whom the Ceremony was performed.
1813 May 30th No. 22	Charles Fortunatus Freeman	Born of Parents unknown	African names			C. J. Chapman Minister
May 30th No. 23	Paulo Leando	Born of Parents unknown	African names	St Peter's Mancroft		Rev. C. J. Chapman Minister
May 30th No. 24	Edward Makenzie	Born of Parents unknown	African names	St Peters Mancroft		Rev. C. J. Chapman Minister

apprehended, this little history contains matter well worthy of the notice and attention of every Christian reader'.

Olaudah Equiano, (c.1745-1797), probably born in Benin, was also captured by slavers, and taken across the Atlantic. Clearly an exceptional man, he impressed his various owners and was eventually freed. His autobiography, *An Interesting Narrative of the life of Olaudah Equiano or Gustavus Vassa the African* was first published in London in 1789 (Vassa was a name assigned to him by one of his owners during his slavery). It was the first book to give a description of the horrors of the 'Middle Passage', the journey across the Atlantic on board a slave ship. It was taken up by anti-slavery campaigners and nine editions were published over the next five years, including one in Norwich paid for by his supporters, whose names are given in the front of the book.

Ignatius Sancho (1729-1780) was actually born at sea during a journey in the Middle Passage – which neither of his parents survived. He was brought up in Greenwich where he eventually found refuge with the Duke and Duchess of Montague. Sancho wrote music and entertained within literary circles, and his letters, published posthumously, were widely read in English abolitionist circles. Many of them were to William Stevenson, the Norwich newspaper proprietor, and a dedicated abolitionist. One of the letters, which were published in 1782, contains a condemnation of the slave trade then practised by the British and most European countries. To John Wingrave, (a London bookseller); 'I am sorry to observe that the practice of your country (which as a resident I love—and for its freedom—and for the many blessings I enjoy in it—shall ever have my warmest wishes—prayers—and blessings); I say it is with reluctance, that I must observe your country's conduct has been uniformly wicked in the East—West-Indies—and even on the coast of Guinea.—The grand object of English navigators—indeed of all Christian navigators—is money—money—money'.

The work of men like these, and their supporters in Norwich and elsewhere, led to the abolition of the slave trade by Britain in 1807. After this date, British ships patrolled the Atlantic, capturing ships of other countries that contained slaves and setting them free: the freed slaves usually went to Sierra Leone to start a new life. A small number, too young to fend for themselves, were brought back to Britain, a special form of refugee: slave children who had been taken from their parents in Africa to be shipped across the Atlantic Ocean. Three such boys were baptised in the font at St Peter Mancroft church on 30 May 1813. They were given the names of Paulo Loando, Edward Mackenzie, and Charles Fortunatus Freeman. We do not know what their African names had been, and we do not know what happened to them in later life. They emerge from the anonymity of the past for just this one brief moment in this Norwich church almost 200 years ago.

COTTON AND CHARLEY

Other black and minority ethnic residents of Norwich include the two men known only as 'Cotton' and 'Charley' painted by John Dempsey in the 1820s, whose portraits are now in the Tasmanian Museum and Art Gallery. One black 'vagrant' who died in the Bridewell was Samuel Turner, a native of Martinique in the West Indies: he was 69 years old when on 29 January 1819 he was confined, 'in a very weak state of health, being troubled with a spitting of blood, and languished until Thursday [11] February when he died'. There were black servants in the city, too, such as William Darby, apparently a butler in a house on All Saints' Green, and Joseph Diana, servant to Robert Herring in Bracondale. Diana later moved to a new employer in north Norfolk and was sentenced to seven years transportation for theft at Fakenham assizes in 1792. He must have been one of the first people of African origin to reach the Australian continent.

Darby married a white woman, Mary Stamps, and their son has a unique claim to fame, surely the only Norwich-born person mentioned in a Beatles lyric! In 1967 John Lennon saw an old poster in an antique shop in Sevenoaks in Kent. It advertised a circus entertainment in Rochdale in 1843 and gave the name Pablo Fanque:

> *PABLO FANQUE'S CIRCUS ROYAL, TOWN MEADOWS ROCHDALE. GRANDEST NIGHT OF THE SEASON! AND POSITIVELY THE LAST NIGHT BUT THREE! BEING FOR THE BENEFIT OF MR KITE (LATE OF WELLS'S CIRCUS) AND MR J HENDERSON, THE CELEBRATED SOMERSET THROWER, WIRE DANCER, VAULTER, RIDER ETC...*

Charley, a Norwich shoe salesman in the 1820s, painted by John Dempsey in 1823.
© Collection: Tasmanian Museum and Art Gallery.

Lennon was so entranced he put most of the text of the poster into his song 'Being for the Benefit of Mr Kite!' on the Beatles' album 'Sergeant Pepper's Lonely Hearts Club Band', one of the best-selling albums of all time. Lennon could not know it, but Fanque was the first black circus proprietor in Britain: he was also Norwich-born. His real name was William Darby, son of William and Mary Darby, and born, probably in Norwich Workhouse, in 1810.

Pablo Fanque's blue plaque, born in Norwich and the first black British circus proprietor.

Darby was Britain's first black circus proprietor but there were many other immigrants from all over the world among circus folk. One was 'Maccomo', known as 'the black lion tamer'. His real name was Arthur Williams and he was a West Indian sailor, perhaps continuing in the traditions of the black sailors who can be seen in paintings of the death of Admiral Nelson: one Norfolk newspaper account describes him as a 'Zulu', referring to his African origins. Maccomo had the misfortune to be attacked by one of the lions he was taming at Manders's Circus in Norwich in the Christmas season in 1862. He survived to continue his career, returning to Norwich in 1867. He died in Sunderland in 1871.

Another black resident in Victorian Norwich was Alexander Merrick Fuller. His father was Joseph Jackson Fuller, born the son of slave parents in Spanish Town, Jamaica, in 1825. Joseph married Elizabeth Johnson, a Jamaican schoolteacher apparently of Sierra Leone origin, and they had three children, one of whom was Alexander who was born in 1849 in Bimbia, Cameroon. Joseph worked as a Baptist missionary in the Cameroon for many years and, after his first wife died, married Charlotte Diboll a missionary from a Norfolk family, in 1861. The family links with Norfolk brought Fuller here, and he set up Alexander as an apprentice in a Norwich engineering firm. In 1871, the family was living in Rupert Street. The census of that year lists Charlotte, Alexander (described as an engine fitter), and Joseph, Charlotte's own son, born in about 1866. Alexander stayed in the city for many years after his apprenticeship, marrying Sophia Mace in 1874: they had six children in the city.

INDIAN IMMIGRANTS

There were a small number of immigrants from the Indian subcontinent in Norwich. In 1881, a man known only as Abdullah was living in the house of John Mitchell in St John Timberhill. He was 24 years old and had been born in Lahore, India. He is described as 'butler, unemployed' so was presumably staying there while looking for a new situation. A longer-term resident in the Victorian city was John Sumser Ali, born in Calcutta, India, and working in Norwich as a gardener. He married a Norfolk 'gal' in Norwich in 1856, when he was 23 years old. He remained in Norwich all his life, dying in the city in 1911.

One man from the Indian subcontinent was in Norwich in 1893 and bought direct gains to several inhabitants of the city. His name was Karim Bakhsh, sometimes spelled Kraem Bocesh, and he practised in the city as an oculist (eye specialist), having practised in Bradford for nine years. In the summer of 1893, Kream Bocesh from the Punjab was offering eye cures from his house at 6 Valentine Street off Dereham Road: 'May be consulted daily from 10 until 1 and from 2 until 8. Working men at any time most convenient for them-selves. Half-charge to people in very poor circumstances… This East Indian Medicine is good for all diseases of the Eye. I have Testimonials from France, Spain, Italy, Austria; also England and India'. The advertisements quoted a testimonial from a local girl, Hannah Reeve: this was no fake and Hannah was prepared to travel to London to support Bocesh when the time came.

His story came to light when he was one of four Indian oculists brought to trial accused of defrauding people by pretending to heal eye diseases in towns across England: the case was brought by the London and Counties Medical Protection Association, and was held at the Old Bailey from 24 October 1893. However, the three witnesses who came down from Norwich to appear in the case at the Old Bailey were all unstinting in their praise of the work of the Indian oculist. The evidence they gave is tribute to the openness and tolerance of Norwich people in their willing acceptance of the benefits of 'foreign' skills.

William Ralph lived in Distillery Road, and was a watch-maker and jeweller, so good eyesight was vital to his work. His right eye had begun to fail 12 years earlier, and after 10 years he had lost sight in it entirely: a local doctor had said there was no cure. In the summer of 1892, his left eye started to fail in just the same way. Both eyes were extremely painful. He went to the oculists, and was operated on by an Indian assistant, named Sunda: 'I can see very well now, very much better than I could before I went to the Indians—Sunda examined my eyes, and told me there was no cure for the sight of my right eye, but that he could stay the pain in it.... I attended twice a day, and I am still under their treatment—the sight of the left eye has been improving every day—I have lost all pain from both eyes'.

There were two other witnesses from Norwich. Hannah Reeve – who we have already mentioned – was an 18-year-old brush-maker, who lived in Heigham, close to the oculists' surgery: she had become completely blind. She had tried a local doctor and the City Eye Infirmary, who gave her powders and drops for many weeks to no avail. James Palmer, a sand-shifter of Barrack Street, could see nothing out of the right eye and only a little with the left eye: he had tried a chemist and the Eye Infirmary with no success. Hannah had been recommended to the Indian oculists by a friend, Palmer's sister had been given a flyer issued by them in the street. Like Ralph, they had been treated by Sunda and were able to see thanks to his treatment. Hannah said, 'I can see in both eyes now—I can go about Norwich without being led, and I can lead other patients about now'. Palmer had been able to return to his work. The Judge in the case made a statement all immigrants on trial would like to hear: 'These men, as foreigners, are entitled to the same justice of law as any English subject'. All the men were acquitted: these immigrants, especially Kraem Bocesh, with the skills they had brought, had been of direct – almost miraculous – benefit to people in Norwich. Unfortunately they had used up all their money in fighting the case and returned to India.

DULEEP SINGH

Perhaps the most well-known immigrant from the Indian subcontinent to Norfolk died at about the same time as Bocesh was practising in Norwich: this was the Maharajah Duleep Singh. Born in the Punjabi royal family in 1838, he was proclaimed Maharajah of the Punjab in 1843, but forced to renounce his throne by the British and live in exile among them: he arrived in Britain in 1854. His residence from 1863 was Elveden Hall near Thetford, where he became a prominent member of the 'hunting, shooting and fishing' community in the county, rated the fourth best shot in Britain and known as 'the Black Prince'. He never gave up hope of restoration as ruler of his home country, which incurred British displeasure. Dying in Paris, he is buried at Elveden and there is a statue to him in the town of Thetford, both places of pilgrimage to members of the Sikh community throughout the world. The local newspaper summed up an important aspect: 'an exile from his native land and from the throne of his forefathers, he was led to brood in consequence upon what he regarded as his wrongs'.

Two of his children – second-generation immigrants – also made their mark. Sophia Duleep Singh was a well-known suffragette: she also visited Indian troops fighting for Britain on the Western Front in the First World War. Prince Frederick Duleep Singh became a local historian and collector of manuscripts especially old maps. These are now in the Norfolk Record Office, preserved thanks to his energy and enthusiasm for his adopted county.

Other Indians in the city included entertainers, some travelling to Britain on their own initiative, others engaged in India by British entrepreneurs. One group of 18 strolling players from Oudh in north east India were engaged by British entrepreneurs in Bombay in 1867, coming to Britain and playing in London and then in Norwich. Matters came to a head while they were in Norwich: they had been badly treated and not received their share of the profits from the shows. Eleven of them – four men, three women and four children – fled by train to London, winding up at a 'Strangers' Home for Asians, Africans and South Sea Islanders' in London. The India Office eventually paid for their return to India.

JENNY LIND

CHAPTER 7

Incomers from Europe in the 18th and 19th Centuries

There were many other immigrants from Europe in the 18th and 19th centuries, some more to be regarded as visitors, others establishing roots that continued for generations.

Opposite: Jenny Lind, Swedish singer and benefactress to Norwich.

One short term immigrant who has left his identity as the name of a public house was 'The Wild Man'. His story is told in the local press describing a major fire in the Bridewell (adjoining the present pub) on 22 October 1751: 'At the time of the fire, there was a man of about forty years of age confined in the Bridewell, who had been taken up as a stroller about two months before; he had remarkable wildness in his look, and a very long beard; and what is most astonishing, he was so far from endeavouring an escape, although the whole building was in flames, that it required force to remove him. On any question being asked, he would answer by a confused inarticulate noise, nor could it ever be made out where he came from, 'till the following advertisement appeared in the London Evening Post; in consequence of which he was removed as therein directed: Lost or strayed away, from Broadway in the parish of Northchurch, near Berkhamstead in the county of Hertford, about three months ago, Peter the Wild Youth, a black hairy man, about five feet eight inches high; he cannot speak to be understood, but makes a kind of humming noise and answers in that manner to the name of Peter'.

He was first found at about Christmas 1725, in the woods near Hamelin in Germany – 'a creature of human kind, naked and wild, being a boy about twelve or thirteen years old. When he was first discovered, he was so wild and savage as to shun all human kind, and could climb up the trees with an agility scarcely to be conceived'. An enforced immigrant, he was brought to England as a kind of entertainment for the royal family, being sent to work at the farm at Berkhamstead when they became bored with him.

GERMAN IMMIGRANTS

One house in Redwell Street was occupied by two successive immigrants in the later 18th century, each bringing their own contribution to city life. In the 1770s it was occupied by John Christopher Hampp, a cloth merchant from Germany. He also dealt in stained glass, particularly medieval glass from former monastic houses, which he imported from Europe, buying it in Rouen, the Rhineland, Nuremberg and the Netherlands. The largest single collection came from the former monastery of Steinfeld, some of which is at Blickling Hall (whose Dutch-style gables of 1624 are among the earliest in the county – this Norfolk treasure house embraces many influences from abroad over the centuries). The glass was fitted into many churches in Norfolk: some of it still survives, for example at Chedgrave, Earsham and Hingham, another European legacy to the county. One example that can be seen in the city is the image of St Brice in the window of the south ambulatory in Norwich Cathedral: he is represented as an archbishop, holding a double cross. This is glass made in Rouen in about 1600 and brought to Norwich by Hampp. He acted as a deacon of the French Church in 1809, and died in Norwich in 1825.

Around 1783, Hampp moved out of Redwell Street, to a 'better' address, in Surrey Street Mews. His place was taken by Mr Dufresnoy, a French teacher, who had previously lived at Strangers' Hall. Trade directories and local newspapers feature many similar men and women, earning their living by teaching European languages to Norwich people.

ITALIAN IMMIGRANTS

Artists of many kinds were also attracted to the city, adding to its cosmopolitan mix. Groups of Italians were especially common. A Nonconformist minister visiting the city, Mr Marten, was accosted in a city street in 1825 by 'two Italian Image lads', trying to sell paintings and busts of famous figures. An educated man, he surprised them by speaking in their language. They were originally from Florence, and had walked to Norwich from London carrying their goods on their heads: the journey had taken them five days. These makers and sellers of small statuettes and figurines were known as figurinai and came principally from one area of Italy, the province of Lucca. In Italy the statues were mainly of saints, but they soon adapted to local tastes and produced images of popular national and local heroes. Typically there might be one padrone controlling six boys who did the actual selling. One such 'patron' was Dominico Crostea of Norwich who employed a lad called Giuliano Mantova to travel about the county with the images. We know of Mantova only because Crostea was involved in a court case in Norwich after an incident in Aylsham in 1822: no doubt there were many similar immigrants whose names have not come down to us.

Another Italian immigrant, Giovanni Bianchi, is described in the 1845 trade directory as a modeller and in later directories as a plaster figure maker: his studio was at St George's Bridge Street. His wife was a Great Yarmouth girl, Sarah Rivett, and their first child, Alesandro was born there in about 1839, so Bianchi probably lived there for a while after his arrival in England in about 1836. They were in Norwich by 1841 where their second daughter, Maria and their youngest son, Fillipo were born, their names showing a pride in Bianchi's Italian background. They had further children, some of whom died in infancy, but four grew up to have families of their own. Bianchi died in 1872, aged 64: his widow then moved to London where she died five years later.

Pellegrino Mazzotti was also from Lucca. A figure maker and modeller, he exhibited works in exhibitions held by the Norwich School of Art between 1821 and 1829. In 1822, he married Mary Leeds in St John Maddermarket: they had four daughters between 1822 and 1827. His first studio was in Strangers' Hall in 1819, his second in Goat Lane. He deserted his family in about 1840, moving to Cambridge. Mary died in Norwich in 1861, and Mazzotti himself died in poverty in the Union Workhouse in Wisbech, Cambridgeshire, in 1879.

View of Norwich by Dutch School, c.1707 – Norwich seen through Dutch eyes. © Norfolk Museums and Archaeology Service.

ARTISTS

Painting was well represented too, at least two German-born immigrants brought their skills into the city. Lewis Hubner (1694-1767) was one, specialising in still-life pictures. Better known is John Theodore Heins, who came to Norwich in about 1720 and stayed in the city for the rest of his life. His paintings include several of the official portraits of the mayors of Norwich, portraits of Mary Chapman and the trustees of the Bethel Hospital, as well as a self-portrait now in the Castle museum and an altar piece of the Resurrection: originally in St Michael Coslany church, this can now be seen, still in its original frame, in Trowse church. Like other works of his, it is signed 'D Heins', the D standing for Dietrich, the German equivalent of Theodore. Heins died in Norwich in 1756: his son, also John Theodore Heins, worked in London in the later decades of the 18th century. A female artist also played a role in the cultural achievements of the city: the oval sitting room at St Helen's House, part of the Great Hospital, has decorative murals by Angelica Kauffman, who worked in England from 1766 to 1781. She had been born in Chur in Switzerland, and spent several years in Rome before coming to England, where she exhibited many paintings at the Royal Academy in London, then a fairly uncommon achievement for a female artist. After about 20 years in England, she moved back to Italy, dying in Rome in 1807.

Collectors who brought foreign culture into the city included the Harvey family and the Pattesons, collectors of paintings including Italian, Dutch and Flemish works: John Patteson's collection was sold by Christie's the

Opposite: *Self Portrait* by J T Heins, 1726. © Norfolk Museums and Archaeology Service.

auctioneers on his death in 1819: it included paintings by the Amsterdam painter, Peter Tillemans. These wealthy Norwich merchants had strong links with Europe. Patteson's mother was Martha Fromanteel, of Dutch descent, while Thomas Harvey, who was a patron of John Crome, married Anne Twiss, daughter of an English merchant who lived in Rotterdam. He bought many of his paintings from a firm in Antwerp. Artists of the Norwich School of Art found their inspiration in Dutch paintings which they could see in these merchant houses, Crome for example regarding the Dutch artist Meindert Hobbema as his master.

Another collection of European importance to find a home in the city was that of the great Swedish botanist, Carl Linnaeus. His library and natural history were purchased by the Norwich botanist James Edward Smith in 1788: the King of Sweden, recognising the iconic nature of the material, is said to have sent a ship to try to prevent the passage of it to Norwich, but he was too late. Smith resided in one of the large terrace houses still to be seen in Surrey Street close to the present bus station, dying here in 1828.

CLOCK-MAKERS

More clock-makers and jewellers from Europe brought their skills into the city in the 18th and 19th centuries. Simon Langanbaker advertised in the Norwich Mercury in 1765: 'Lately arrived from Germany. Great variety of wooden Clocks and Alarms… with the Cuckoos who sing to Admiration'. Lorenz Beha was a German Roman Catholic who came to Norfolk from Baden Baden in 1833. He worked in King's Lynn for over a decade, but was in Norwich by 1847, based at St Stephen's Plain, with his brother Matthias and a younger immigrant also from Baden Baden, Dominick Lickert: all three were watch and clock-makers. Beha was robbed and murdered in 1853, the murderer stealing from him two silver watches worth £15 as well as cash: a William Thompson was hanged for the crime in the following year.

Four members of the Zipfel family appear to have moved from Germany and settled in Norwich in the early years of the 19th century, all working as clock and watch-makers. One was Charles Zipfel, who arrived in the city in about 1800 and married Editha Morris in Norwich in 1807. An advertisement in the Norfolk Chronicle for 1807 reads: 'C Zipfel of Germany having entered upon the sign of 'the Hand' at the bottom of Elm Hill, earnestly solicits the patronage of his friends and the public in general, assuring them that every exertion shall be made for their comfort and accommodation. NB Clocks of all sorts are made, sold and repaired, as at his former residence, the Lion and Castle, Timberhill'.

Their son Charles, also a clock-maker, worked in Magdalen Street – the street name Zipfel's Court shows where – and his four children were all apprentices in the business. Successive generations of the family carried on the business until 1938 when it was taken over by Albert Symonds, himself a member of the family: his mother was Catherine Agnes, née Zipfel. There were other branches of the family in the city: the 1845 trade directory has three Zipfels, at St Gregory's, Ber Street and Stump Cross.

Four generations of another immigrant family, the Rossis, operated a gold- and silver-smith's shop in Norwich, at first in Exchange Street, later in Guildhall Hill. The founder was George Rossi, born in Italy who had fought for Napoleon before settling in Norwich in 1815. His wife's name was Elizabeth and they had seven children baptised in St Peter Mancroft church between 1836 and 1849. Rossi died in 1865: his son, Theodore, took over the business, which finally closed in 1936 on the retirement of the last member of the family.

JENNY LIND

The world of entertainment and sport has also produced many talents from all across the world, who have graced the city with their skills, and in some cases provided a permanent legacy, none greater than that of Jenny Lind. Born in Stockholm in 1820, Lind began to sing on stage when she was ten. At the age of 20, she was a member of the Royal Swedish Academy of Music and court singer to the King of Sweden and Norway. She toured Denmark where, in 1843, Hans Christian Anderson fell in love with her; after she rejected him, he is supposed to have portrayed her as the Snow Queen, with a heart of ice. In July 1847, Lind starred in the world première of Verdi's opera I Masnadieri.

Lind's devotion to charitable causes was a key aspect of her career and greatly enhanced her international popularity even among the unmusical.

She appeared in Norwich for the first time at St Andrews' Hall on 22, 23 and 25 September 1847: her fee was £1,000, of which she gave £200 to city charities. She stayed at the Bishop's Palace as the guest of the Bishop. In January 1849 she gave two more concerts for local charities at the same venue: this time she waived her fee and more than £3,000 was raised. She wanted the money spent on a new charity of lasting benefit to the people of Norwich, and eventually (after rejecting an original proposal for public baths), it was decided to build an infirmary for sick children. Had the proposal been put into action straight away, the Jenny Lind might have been the first children's hospital in England, but due to the delays it was the fourth. Two concerts in February 1856 followed, and she appeared for the final time in April 1862. A bust in her honour was unveiled at the Jenny Lind Infirmary by Madame Albani in September 1894: Emma Albani, a Canadian-born singer, had herself appeared many times at the Norwich festival from 1872 and had given a concert in aid of the Infirmary in November 1885.

The Jenny Lind Hospital was originally in Pottergate, later moving to its better-known site on the Unthank Road, after J J Colman gave the land in honour of his late wife. Money raised at Queen Victoria's jubilee was also put into the new hospital, which was opened by the Prince and Princess of Wales in June 1900. This too has now closed, but the name of this Swedish singer is still honoured: the children's ward of the Norfolk and Norwich University Hospital is named for Jenny Lind. As she herself wrote in 1885, 'of all the money God allowed me to give away when my poor throat could call an audience to listen to its production, none had borne a nobler and more genuine fruit than the Jenny Lind Hospital in Norwich'.

ENTERTAINERS

Short term visitors had less lasting effects on the city than Jenny Lind, but added to the variety of life within the city. In the days before television, anything out of the ordinary would attract a crowd: to be unusually tall or short was to be an attraction, and to be 'foreign' added to the exotic appeal. Such showmen included 'O'Brien, the Irish giant' who showed himself at Norwich over Christmas in 1790. This was not the Patrick O'Brien who died in 1783 and whose skeleton is on display in the Hunterian Museum in London, but Patrick Cotter, another Irishman, who took on the name after the death of the original 'Irish Giant'. Cotter himself was supposed to be eight feet three inches tall (2.44 metres). He died in Bristol in 1806, and had his body buried in an exceptionally deep vault to prevent any possible grave-robbing; these people, seen as 'freaks' in their time, were given no peace, even in death.

A Polish immigrant, 'Count' Joseph Boruwlaski, lived for some while in St Stephen's in Norwich in 1788. Born in Poland in 1739, he never grew more than 39 inches (0.99 metre) tall. Although occasionally reduced to showing himself, he generally managed to support himself by giving guitar concerts in his rooms. He later moved to Durham, where he died in 1837 at the age of 97. In his autobiography, he acknowledges the kind support of an unnamed Norwich lady during his stay in the city. A later 'dwarf' to entertain the people of Norwich was the legendary Tom Thumb, who appeared at the Theatre Royal in 1844.

Superstars at Norwich over the weekend of 21-22 September 1840 impressed the Norfolk Chronicle as 'four of the greatest performers of the century': they were M Liszt, Madame Persiani, Signor Rubini and Signor Puzzi, playing in concerts at the Theatre Royal and the Assembly Rooms. This early Victorian equivalent of a rock festival must have been a great moment in the city, but only the name of Liszt is remembered today.

RELIGION AND MEDICINE

Faith continued to break through national barriers. The Roman Catholic community at Notre Dame in Surrey Street is a good example, a teaching order first brought to the city in 1864. In 1901, to take just one date at random, the members of the community included five born in

Ireland, one in Bombay, India, one in Australia and one in New Orleans in the United States, while the young pupils staying with them included a 15-year-old born in Germany and a ten-year-old born in Trinidad, Port of Spain. The first nuns had stayed at Strangers' Hall for eight months while their new home was being made ready, yet another case where this building has housed incomers.

Dr Allan Minns, Mayor of Thetford 1904-1906.

Medicine also transcended national boundaries. One late 19th century incomer was Dr Harrington Wyndham Darrell, born in Bermuda in the West Indies of white parents in 1863, who came to Norwich and practised medicine in the city. He was in Norwich in 1891, staying at the house of Robert Mills, surgeon, in Surrey Street. By 1901 he was living at 12 All Saints' Green which was also his surgery. A man of wide interests, he also owned a stable of trotting horses. He died in Norwich on 9 January 1920: a memorial was erected to him in the Cattle Market and more recently moved to a much more prominent site, near the bus stops on Castle Meadow. Many people waiting for the bus to the University must have noticed his name and wondered about his history.

Contemporary with Darrell was the Minns family, born in the Bahamas of a white father and a black mother. Two brothers, Pembroke and Allan, both came to England to be trained as doctors and practised in Thetford: Allan has the distinction of being the first black person to become a mayor of any English town, serving as mayor of Thetford for two years 1904-6. The brothers lived in Thetford for many decades, but Pembroke does have a direct link with Norwich: he died in Sunnyside Nursing Home on Rosary Road on 31 March 1912.

CHAPTER 8

The Traveller Community

We have seen the unique presence of Romani DNA in a skeleton dating from before the Norman Conquest, but the traveller community does not show up in documentary sources until five centuries later: they were generally called 'Egyptians', as they were supposed to have originated in that country, and they are occasionally mentioned under that name: a group of 'Egyptians' were in Norwich in 1544 for example, staying at the house of a Mr Debney.

Opposite: Travellers' caravans at Lakenham, painted by G Colman Green, early 20th century.

One man who brought the traveller lifestyle into people's awareness was George Borrow. Born in Dereham in 1803, his mother was of a Huguenot family, and they lived for many years in a house on Cow Hill in Norwich. His association with travellers later became so close that some people thought he must have had traveller blood, a rumour heard even by the American writer Nathaniel Hawthorne. Borrow met Ambrose (also known as Jasper) Petulengro when he was young, and learned the ways of travellers – and their language – in the traveller camp on Mousehold Heath. It was here he was given the name of 'Lavengro', meaning 'Word-Master'.

This was the origin of one of his most famous pieces of writing, a conversation between Petulengro and Borrow:

Life is sweet, brother
Do you think so?

Think so! There's night and day, brother, both sweet things; sun, moon and stars, brother, all sweet things; there's likewise the wind on the heath. Life is very sweet, brother; who would wish to die
I would wish to die

You talk like a gorgio – which is the same as talking like a fool – were you a Romany Chal you would talk wiser. Wish to die, indeed!
A Romany Chal would wish to live for ever!

Mousehold Heath, where traveller families lived.

Borrow was best known in his lifetime for his book *The Bible in Spain* but is now better remembered for his descriptions of the traveller community in his two books *Lavengro* and *Romany Rye* which describe his encounters on a journey made through Britain in 1825, travelling with just a bundle and a stick. His very first book, *The Zincali* (published in 1841), describes the traveller community in Spain, and in the introduction he says: 'Throughout my life the Gypsy race has always had a peculiar interest for me. Indeed I can remember no period in which the mere mention of the name of Gypsy did not awaken within me feelings hard to be described. I cannot account for this: I merely state a fact'. There is some doubt as to how accurate Borrow's

Right: St Giles' St, Tuck's Court – in his youth George Borrow worked in Solicitors' offices on the east side of Tuck's Court.

descriptions are – and some people he talked to may have strung him along – but he brought awareness of the traveller way of life to many people for the first time.

Because of its connection with Borrow, the family tree of Petulengro was studied a century ago by the Gypsy Lore Society. Several members of the family had Norwich links: laini, or Phoebe, married Tom Cooper of Thorpe, one of their children, Lydia married Tom Brown but died in a fire at Lakenham in 1908. One member of the family was himself a writer – George Smith, born on Mousehold Heath in 1833, was the author of *Incidents in a Gypsy's Life*. He married Kerlenda Lee and one of the children, Alice, was also born on Mousehold Heath, being christened in Catton church.

Another well-known Norwich figure who could have had traveller connections was Jem Mace: Norfolk born, and for a time landlord of the White Swan public house in the city, he is often known as 'the father of modern boxing'. His fighting talents and his friendly association with the members of the traveller community, gave rise to the rumour that he had traveller blood, but he always denied this. However, there were some connections; Mace first fought as 'the Swaffham Gypsy', later just as 'the Gypsy', and members of his family certainly married into the traveller community. A recent biographer, Graham Gordon, thinks that Jem Mace may have been a quarter Roma on his father's side.

Left: Jem Mace blue plaque, a well-known Norwich figure and world heavyweight champion in 1870.

CHAPTER 9

The Jewish Community in 19th Century Norwich

Jews were admitted into England once more in 1656 under the Commonwealth, and there was a small Jewish community in the city from the 18th century. By far the largest community of Jews was in London, and one way of escape from poverty was through sport, as it was in black communities in America in the 20th century. One of the most famous of these was the boxer Daniel Mendoza, who became British champion: he was in Norwich in 1790 and the *Champion* public house is named in his honour.

Several Jewish families came into Norwich in the late 18th and early 19th centuries. David Soman, a French Jewish emigree, set up a cap-making business in Norwich in 1799, soon converting the firm into a boot and shoe factory. Philip Haldenstein, born in about 1823 in Prussia in Germany, moved to England, married Rachel, David Soman's daughter and developed the factory into a major employer in the city: the factory building in Queen Street can still be seen. Philip died in 1891, aged 82, and was succeeded in the business by his sons Woolfe, who died just five years later, and Alfred. Alfred and his family lived at Thorpe Lodge, now Broadland District Council offices. His son George took on the business after Alfred's death in 1921: he revolutionised shoe-making by being the first to use soles that were stuck onto the shoe rather than sewn on. The firm amalgamated with Bally of Switzerland in 1933.

Opposite: Norwich Synagogue, built in the 19th century on Synagogue Lane off King Street. Destroyed in the Second World War.

Alfred had several daughters, including Joyce, born in 1900, who in 1925 married Johan Rozendaal, a member of the Dutch Jewish community and moved to the Netherlands. When the Germans conquered the Netherlands in the Second World War, the male members of the family were rounded up to be sent to concentration camps, but Joyce made an epic escape from the Netherlands through Europe into Switzerland where she was interned for the remainder of the war.

One of Philip's daughters married into another prominent Jewish family in the city, that of the Samuels: a family tradition was that they were direct descendants of the medieval Jewish community in an unbroken line of faith, but this is difficult to prove. The most famous of the line was Arthur Samuel born in 1872, the eldest son of Benjamin Samuel, a pawnbroker on Timberhill, and his wife Rosetta, formerly Haldenstein. Educated at Norwich Grammar School, he became the first Jewish Lord Mayor of Norwich in 1912-3. He went on to become Conservative MP for Farnham 1918-1937, and a minister in Baldwin's government. He became Sir Arthur Samuel in 1932, and Baron Mancroft in 1937: he died in 1942.

RUSSIAN AND POLISH IMMIGRANTS

The Jewish community in the city grew at the end of the 19th century, when large numbers of Polish Jews fled from that part of Poland controlled by Russia after the introduction of the May Laws in 1882: this was the greater part of what we now call Poland, including Warsaw. Many went to America, others settled in Britain and those who came to Norwich often did so after a period in London. One family of Polish immigrants in the city by 1891 were the Eckers. They started in poverty but their eventual success in the tailoring business provided employment for Norwich people. Lewis Ecker first appeared in the city in 1891, living in a poor tenement in St Saviour's Lane. He was still there five years later, but by 1900 'Lewis and Emanuel Ecker' were outfitters based at 9 St Benedict's, the family home. Lewis (the name is sometimes spelled Louis), his wife Lea, his brother Emanuel all lived here, together with Esther Ecker, 65 years old, the mother of the two boys: all four had been born in Poland. Lewis and Lea became British citizens, but the other two did not. At the time of the 1901 census, Lewis and Lea had five children, all born in the city. The firm continued at 9 St Benedict's into a second generation, being known as Ecker and Son in the 1930s: the building is now a restaurant. By this time, the family had two tailoring outlets in the city: H Ecker and Son were in St George's Street, and Ecker and Sons in the Prince of Wales Road. A poor immigrant family, bringing with them just their skills, and, perhaps, carrying their sowing machines as their means of progress in their new life, had become a firm supplying the needs – and providing employment – for many people in their new city of refuge.

Other members of the Russian/Polish diaspora came to Norwich before 1891. Most of them were also tailors, such as Joseph Finsburg and his wife Harriet, living at 52 Peacock Street, both born in Poland. They spent some time in London before coming to Norwich: their son Reuben was born in Whitechapel in 1887. Living with them in 1891 were seven men and one woman, all born in Poland and all described as tailors: Swev Rosenzweig, Mark Silverman, Hyman Smith, Jacob Remer, Woolf Rudsky, Harris Golstein and Jane Rose. Jane Rose is described as Finsburg's sister: she was single, so had presumably changed her name into a more English form. Another family from Russia/Poland was that of Samuel Harrison and his wife Elizabeth. Living at 21/23 Colegate Street in 1891, they had two children born in Manchester, one in Canada and two in Norwich. With them in 1891 was a visitor, Elias Shapps, also born in Poland. Although the Harrisons and the Finsburgs may have fled Poland with almost nothing, they had made good in their profession of tailoring in England over the years: each family had a live-in servant.

A third family appeared in the city a few years later, that of Barrett Lazarus and his wife Sarah. They were in London in 1891, but by 1901 they lived in St Andrew's Hill in Norwich. They were in their early forties, and Barrett worked as a tailor in his home here. Both had been born in Warsaw. They had eight children living with them, aged between 18 years and just three months – their names were Abraham, Miriam, Leah, Louis, Jack, Woolf, Phoebe and David Lazarus. The six eldest children had been born in London, the two youngest in Norwich. This suggests that Barrett and Lazarus had fled from Warsaw perhaps 20 years earlier, and had settled in London: some time between the birth of Woolf and Phoebe, in the later 1890s, they had moved to Norwich. There were two other people staying in the house, both of whom were also born in Poland, in Lodz – Abel Raphael, a machinist, and Solomon Abraham, a tailor: presumably they were fellow refugees living in Barrett's house, a large one, and working for him.

In the 18th century, the Jewish community worshipped in Tombland Alley. A new synagogue was built in the 19th century off King Street. This building was destroyed in air raids in the Second World War: its memory is preserved in the street name of Synagogue Lane, apparently the only street in Britain with this name and its gateposts moved to the present synagogue on Earlham Road. Norwich is now home to two Jewish congregations and a small but thriving community.

CHAPTER 10

The Early 20th Century

We think of English people travelling abroad as tourists but there was a reverse traffic as well. The years before the First World War saw many foreign visitors to the city, coming from all over the world. Queen Kapiolani of Hawaii and her daughter Princess Liliukani, visited Norwich when they came to England for the celebrations of the jubilee of Queen Victoria. They stayed with Captain and Mrs Steward of Rackheath Hall, who had known them when they had previously lived in Hawaii. The royal party visited the Cathedral, St Andrew's Hall, the Guildhall and St Peter Mancroft, and then went to Pinebanks, the home of John Taylor, where they climbed the tower he used for astronomy: the tower still stands, and the Queen's visit is recorded on a plaque on its wall. August 1900 saw a visit from Prince Pura Chatra of Siam (now Thailand) and his brother, Prince Yugula, who came to the city from Cromer, where they were staying. Another high-status visitor was Gbadebo, the Alake of Abeokuta – a Nigerian prince. He travelled in England in 1904, landing in May at Plymouth, proceeding to London, then onto Norwich, and then to Aberdeen, leaving Britain on 9 July.

Opposite: Statue by Austrian sculptor Joseph Boehm formerly part of the fountain erected by Sir John Boileau, now in the grounds of the former Norfolk and Norwich Hospital.

A very different black visitor to Norwich was Robert Rody, who found himself in Norwich prison for a month in October 1912. A native of Jamaica, he had been living and working in Great Yarmouth over the summer, making money by selling bangles and working as a photographer. One night in September, he and his wife Ellen, a white woman, were walking down Regent Road when they were met by a group of five young men up from London for the races who subjected her to racial abuse for walking out with a black man, and assaulted them. She defended herself with her only weapon, an umbrella, but Rody had a knife and inflicted some wounds on his assailants – for which he was arrested and charged with attempted murder. In late October he was tried in Norwich – where a jury of local men found him NOT GUILTY, recognising that he had only been defending himself and his wife: by their verdict, the Norwich jury showed an understanding of racial issues greatly superior to that of many later juries in cases elsewhere in Britain, and indeed than Great Yarmouth opinion at the time. The *Great Yarmouth Independent* had described Rody as a 'bloodthirsty Creole', while the Great Yarmouth police, when asked if they had not seen the bruises on Rody's body, had replied that you could not see bruises as clearly on a black body as upon a white one. There was no question in that age of a claim for wrongful arrest, or for compensation for having spent a month of his life in gaol for a crime of which he was found to be innocent.

ENTERTAINMENT AND SPORT

Entertainment and sport continued to break through national boundaries. There is a gravestone in the Earlham Cemetery to a Japanese boy, Kiyoshi Hata, who died in the city in 1903. The local press tells the story: 'A little lad of about 10 years of age, one of the troupe of Japanese who about 3 weeks ago commenced a fortnight's engagement at Gilbert's Circus died early on Saturday morning from brain fever. He was taken ill early in his first week here, and his feats were thereupon performed by one of the female members of the troupe. He received the best possible treatment, Dr Barton-Fanning being placed in charge of the case, and the troupe remained in Norwich to watch over their little comrade. The interment took place early yesterday morning at the Cemetery'. According to the Norwich death returns, he died at 27 Cattle Market Street. This address is the house next to the present Shire Hall Tavern: in 1903, it was a Temperance Hotel run by Mrs Anne Chapman where the troupe was staying. Hata is described on his death certificate as a 'Japanese Acrobatic Artist' and the cause of death is given as tubercular meningitis and epilepsy. The certificate was signed by H W Darrell, himself well travelled as we have seen.

A cricket team made up of 'Australian Aborigines' toured Britain as early as 1868, not only playing cricket but also demonstrating skills in spears and boomerangs, the latter especially

Above left: Rood screen in the Cathedral of St John the Baptist.
Above right: Statue of Sir Samuel Bignold at Surrey House.

sensational as it was new to most of the spectators. They came to Norwich, playing the Carrow Club on 23-24 July: the local paper noted the 'Australians' surprising skill with the bat'! In the summer of 1900, the West Indian cricket team toured Britain, playing a match in Norwich in August: they had an easy victory. Their team included Charles Ollivierre, who was later to become the first West Indian player to be a county professional when he signed for Derbyshire.

The turn of the century also saw some more permanent contributions to the city by immigrants in the form of statues. The lovely statue of a mother and child now in the grounds of the former Norfolk and Norwich Hospital was originally part of a drinking fountain in the road. It is by Joseph Boehm, born in Vienna in 1834, who arrived in England in 1862 becoming a British subject three years later. There are many statues by him in London, where he died in 1890. The statue was put up by Sir John Boileau – of Huguenot origins – in honour of his late sister, whom the figure is supposed to resemble.

The statues of Sir Samuel Bignold and the Bishop Talbot of Oxford on Surrey House, the Aviva building on Surrey Street, are by a French sculptor, Leon-Joseph Chavalliaud. He was born in Reims in 1858, and spent about 15 years in England at the peak of his career. His works include statues at Sefton Park in Liverpool and one of the actress Mrs Siddons in Paddington Green. Like some other immigrants, he eventually did return to his own country, dying in France in 1919. The marble inside Surrey House is from Italy, and was originally intended for Westminster Roman Catholic Cathedral. Another piece of art by immigrants from this period is in the Cathedral of St John the Baptist – the figures on the rood beam are the work of Peter Rendl of Oberammergau, Germany.

PURE QUALITY & DELICIOUS FLAVOU

CHAPTER 11

The Italian Community

There was a well-known Italian community centred on Ber Street from the later 19th century: Ralph Mottram recalled the striking impression they made on him, especially the women, with 'their abundant hair bound with richly coloured scarves'. The community practised what is sometimes called chain migration: Italians who settled in Norwich would invite friends and relatives from their home area in Italy to come over, pay for their transportation, and arrange employment and initial accommodation for them.

Opposite: Pietro Chiesa of Italy and Norwich, ice cream seller. © Norfolk Libraries, Picture Norfolk.

The community has deeper roots than is generally thought: some were already in the city by the middle of the 19th century. In 1851 Joseph Ceseratti was living in Ber Street, with his English-born wife and their four children, also all born in England. It was a large house and boarders there included four other Italians, Augustino Lagoimaerino, Bartolomeo Rogio, Antonio Vacaro and Benedetto Furno. All five men were musicians by profession.

Fifty years later, there were several Italian families in or near Ber Street, including three living in next-door tenements in a yard off Ber Street known as Boarded Entry Yard: the Gizzi and Marcantoni families had probably been in the city about 15 years, judging by the birth-places of the children, while the third, the Parvanis, may have been more recent incomers.

Another household of Italians lived a little away from Ber Street, in St Stephen's Road at the beginning of the 20th century. This was the home of Copolot Linge, his wife Elizabeth, brother-in-law Wentry Linge and sister Rosalba Linge. All four were born in Italy, but had probably been in Norwich over a decade as the two children of Copolot and Elizabeth – ten-year-old Christini and eight-year-old Josephini were both born in the city. Three other Italians lived in the house as lodgers – a widower named Dominaro Cranforone and two single men in their twenties, Loreto Mammone and Antonio Maino. Another Ber Street family was that of Maria Butcher, born in Italy in spite of her English sounding name, and her two male cousins Pasquete and Niscendro Yannitti.

MUSIC

What these families had in common was music: Norwich a century ago must have been alive with the music given to its streets by these immigrants. The men in these families were musicians, generally described as organ grinders or street organ players, the youngest being one of the Marcantonis, who was only 15. One of his teenage sisters is also described as a street organ player (the only female I have seen so described), the other as a street singer. The musical tradition culminated in the career of Antoinette Carrera, later Hannent upon her marriage. Known as 'Black Anna' from her hair and dress she was landlady of the *Jolly Butchers* public house in Ber Street from 1935 until her death in 1975, her style of jazz entertaining many thousands of city residents, including American airmen during the Second World War.

FOOD

Not all members of the Italian community were musicians. Many in the community were involved with the food industry. Cesare Coretta, born in Piedmont in 1879, arrived in England in 1898 and became a fish fryer at Norwich Fisheries. Sisto Reali was selling ice cream in Norwich by 1914, as were Peter Chiesa and Dominici Mancini. Chiesa was known as 'Big Peter' from his height, and had previously been a plasterer, Mancini lived in Prospect Place on Hall Road where his workers included 17-year-old

Anna Hannent, 'Black Anna' of the *Jolly Butchers* public house.

Dominici Cocco, like Mancini himself Italian born.

The two best known families of Italian immigrants are probably the Peruzzi and Valori families. Both were in the city before the First World War, Salvador Peruzzi operating a greengrocers in Heigham Street, while one set of Valori brothers had fried fish shops on Bishop Bridge Street and Magdalen Street, another operating as plasterers on Waterloo Road. Both families had expanded their interests in the city by the time of the Second World War a generation later. The Peruzzis were making ice cream – Salvador at Heigham Street and Derby Street, Joseph at Adelaide Street. The Valoris had five fish shops, including the long-running business on Timberhill, and also sold ice cream at two establishments in the city.

The Second World War was a difficult time for the Italian community as Italy – an ally in the First World War – was an enemy for the first three years of the war. Italian men who had been in Britain less than 20 years were interned, but most Italians in the city had been in Britain much longer than this. Older men – and occasionally women – might also be interned if they were thought to be Fascist sympathisers. There were riots against Italian communities in several British cities when Mussolini declared war in June 1940. However, I have not seen evidence of any trouble in Norwich, and Italian families continued to be welcome in the city. By the 1970s, the Valoris had further fish shops including one on Rose Lane. As is well-known, the Beatles played at the Grosvenor Rooms in Norwich on 17 May 1963: a plaque on the wall records that after the gig the band went for fish and chips at Valori's!

There was an influx of Italian immigrants immediately after the war, when reconstruction schemes required a new workforce. They were mainly women in their early 20s, working as domestic servants and hospital orderlies: there was a large contingent in the city by 1950. Later still, Felix Bernasconi was a third generation immigrant, the grandson of a man who had left Italy in the 1800s. Bernasconi himself was born in London but worked in Jarrold's department store in Norwich from 1945 to 1976. His paintings of local scenes have become increasingly appreciated since his death in 2001.

FOR THE

Belgian Relief Fund

SALE CATALOGUE

(Inaugurated by the City Club, Norwich)

OF

ARTICLES

Given by Norfolk and Norwich Sympathisers

AT THE

AGRICULTURAL HALL ASSEMBLY ROOMS,

At 7 p.m. - January 13th, 1915.

ADMISSION BY CATALOGUE ONLY

Price 3d. each

EVERY LOT TO BE SOLD WITHOUT RESERVE.

CHAPTER 12

The First World War and the 1920s

The First World War produced more refugees to Norwich. Germany's invasion of Belgium in 1914 saw many flee from the country, both native Belgians and members of the 'ex-pat' British community living there.

Opposite: Poster advertising a concert in aid of Belgian refugees.

One of the latter was Mrs W H Newman, whose story was told in the Carrow Works Magazine in January 1915: her experience brought the fate of refugees home to many Norwich readers. The family had lived for 'many happy years' in Antwerp when in August 1914 war broke out and she found herself and her family under immediate threat:

'My husband arrived at home that evening at 7 O'clock, with the news that the children and myself were to leave for England at 9am, and so panic stricken were we all, that it was thought to be the last boat leaving the town, therefore our last chance of getting away.

After talking it over quietly, we decided that the children should leave in the care of our friends, and we immediately started packing, as the luggage had to go on board that night, and many tears were packed in with the clothes'.

The parents stayed on for a few more days, during which many refugees from the countryside flooded into the city:

> *'not one of these refugees came into the town without carrying something or other of their worldly belongings, some even had small handcarts on which furniture and bedding had been piled, and most of the men carried sacks of potatoes or apples on their backs, and the women sheets which contained anything they could pick up and throw in. One poor woman was*

Below and opposite: Images of refugees from Belgium, brought to the attention of Norwich people when the images were printed in the Carrow Works Magazine in 1915.

seen to wander round the town for two days carrying a lamp-shade, evidently her newest purchase; and most of the young girls carried their hats, also a very valuable possession, only worn on high days and holidays. Many had seen their husbands and brothers shot down before their eyes, and all were so stunned with grief and horror of what they had seen, but there were very little outward signs of it'.

One day the family were given just four hours to pack up and go to the harbour. She concluded: 'it will take many years to efface the sensation we had on closing our front door, not knowing if we should ever see anything of our house again'.

Many Belgian refugees arrived on fishing boats at Lowestoft or Great Yarmouth before coming into Norwich: they were looked after by local families, and concerts and other events were held to support former inhabitants of 'gallant little Belgium'. The most well-known such refugee from Belgium to East Anglia, however, is a fictitious character – Hercule Poirot, Agatha Christie's detective who, according to the novels, was looked after at a house in Essex after fleeing his native land. He was based on Belgian refugees Christie had met during nursing work.

One member of an immigrant family who made a major contribution to 20th century life was Louis Marchesi, born in 1898. His father was a Swiss confectioner, his mother Irish. He became a member of Norwich Rotary Club, and then decided to form a similar club, intended exclusively for younger men – he was 27 at the time. Marchesi owned Langford's restaurant in London Street, where the Table held its first meetings. The club was called 'The Round Table': although images of King Arthur and the Knights of the Round Table were not excluded, the actual reason for the name was a speech of the Prince of Wales urging business and professional men to get together round the table to discuss things. Twenty years later, there were over 200 Round Table groups in Britain alone, and almost 40 female groups – 'Ladies' Circles'. He died in Norwich in 1968. The Round Table now operates in 60 countries around the world, undertaking an enormous quantity of charitable work.

CHAPTER 13

The Second World War

The Second World War brought about an enormous dislocation, with huge numbers of people forced to live for many years far away from their homelands: many never returned. Norwich played its full part in these movements.

Opposite: Norwich Cathedral, as painted by Danish-born artist Ludwig Lund, official artist to the American Second Air Division in the Second World War.

CHILD REFUGEES

The Spanish Civil War was the first of these dislocations: the Labour Party's May Day celebration in Norwich Market Place in 1938 included Spanish refugee children. As the *Eastern Daily Press* noted, there were 36 Basque boys and girls 'some of them in dresses of their national colours and headed by a Spanish republican flag… they sang the Internationale and songs of their country, and one of their number, a girl of fourteen, made a speech in Spanish which was afterwards interpreted to the crowd'. At least one Spanish girl was already in Norwich: Carmen du Zulueta was a pupil at the Blyth school. She spent the summer holiday of 1938 helping her compatriots, noting that 'all the children seemed happy, but they were always thinking of their families and homes, and hoping for the postman to come. The noise of his motor bike at the gate of 'Basque House' (in Colchester, where 57 child refugees were staying) was the signal for them to run to the gate, although they knew that the letters had to go to the staff first, for all the letters from Spain were read beforehand in case they should contain terrible news'.

Like any other group of incomers, they found some customs of their new homeland strange: 'the children had never before seen a man wash-up or scrub and this struck them as extremely funny'. She reported the experience to the Blyth School magazine, with words that hopefully have applied to many groups of refugees coming to Norwich: 'the children left Spain at a time when they could have hardly any food, and no rest, and came to England where people received them with the greatest kindness and gave them all they needed'.

A better-known group of child refugees are the those known as the Kindertransporte, young Jewish boys and girls put onto trains in Germany and German-occupied Austria by their parents, hoping that their loved ones would be safe from the persecution practised by the Nazi regime. In December 1938, 420 Jewish refugee children arrived in East Anglia. They were between seven and 17 years old and had come from Vienna. They crossed the Channel from the Hook of Holland, arriving at Harwich from where they were taken by train to Lowestoft and on to Pakefield Holiday Camp, their temporary residence until permanent homes could be found for them, each child wore a label with his or her name upon it. One girl described her experiences to the local press: she had witnessed the sacking and burning of synagogues and the destruction of Jewish-owned shops in Vienna.

The *Eastern Daily Press* expressed the views of most local people: 'it is with mingled sorrow and pride that one reads of their arrival – sorrow at the irrational and cruel persecution which is the cause of their exile, pride that this free, tolerant and merciful country of ours should be able to provide a refuge for them. Their presence here is in itself a vivid appeal to all who can do so to help the work which is being done in Norwich and the district both to raise funds for the maintenance of the refugees and to find adoptive homes for as many as possible of the children – it would be foreign to all the kindly and merciful traditions of British men and women if means were not found also to give some help to these little fugitives of terror'.

Norwich people rose to the occasion. Mariam Cohen recalled attending a meeting in the city at which it was asked, 'Any offers to take children?' Mariam and her husband Percy 'felt you wanted to do something'. They took Kurt Fuchel, born in Vienna in 1931: he soon settled in, but his fears surfaced at the end of each day: 'every night when it was dark, he'd come down the stairs and he'd see the door was locked'.

These children went to local schools and many Norwich people who were children at the time have memories of them. One of the refugees was Hertha Fischer. She was sponsored by the local branch of the National Council of Women: they were able to raise a guaranteed £62. 14s. 10d. a year, with possible further donations, which, in good English fashion, included the proceeds of 'an annual whist drive'. Hertha was originally sent to a boarding school in north Norfolk, but when this was evacuated to the south of England, she was brought back to Norwich, staying at Anguish's School, Lakenham, from where she attended the Blyth School as a day pupil. Hertha herself contrasted the two country's school systems in an article in the school magazine:

I had heard it was a very strict place, and found it surprisingly different, because when I heard 'strict', I thought of my school in Vienna, which was quite unlike The Blyth School. In Vienna, if you speak one word in the lesson, and are unlucky enough to be caught by the mistress, she will tell you to copy out three pages from a book and write underneath why you had the punishment. This has to be signed by your parents.

I did not mind writing out three pages, but I did mind having to ask my father for his signature, because he got very fierce and thought it very unnecessary to have deserved the punishment.

The homework is very differently arranged too. At the Blyth Secondary School people grumble often enough, because they have two hours' homework! But I think them lucky when I think of the Austrian schoolgirls. In Vienna, it happens that one sometimes gets homework for five subjects, or even more, on one night, because the mistress does not ask whether you have had homework, but just gives it, expecting it to be done, whether you sit up for it till 9 O'clock or 12 midnight.

On Saturday, every school in Vienna works as usual until 12 noon, and then they think themselves very, very lucky to have the afternoon free. It surprised me very much that schools in England should have the whole of Saturday off, for it seemed to me most unusual.

The time when English schools begin their lessons, also seemed to me peculiar, because in Vienna at a quarter to eight, all the children have to be at school ready to begin work; while here some people are lucky enough to be still in bed at that time.

Norwich High School for Girls took in two refugees without payment – and a further eleven had their fees paid for by local families. One was twelve-year-old Franziska Bettelheim, whose brother Freddie also came to Norwich. Another was Lisbeth Weiss, who stayed with the Brenners in Unthank Road and went to the High School with her hosts' daughter, who remembered her as having 'large brown eyes, a tiny suitcase and a little English'. Lisbeth's parents used to telephone her every week but this came to an end, naturally upsetting Lisbeth very much: 'she sat on a little chair with a towel on her head'. She was comforted by the rabbi and eventually her uncle and aunt were able to get out of Vienna, and take Lisbeth with them to a new life in the United States.

ADULT REFUGEES

It was not just the children of course: many adults fled from persecution in Nazi Germany, some coming to Norfolk. The most well-known was the scientist Albert Einstein, who spent some time in Runton before finding a permanent new home in the United States. One who came to Norwich was Franz Eichenberg, a lawyer from Hamburg. A Lutheran himself, he had a mostly Jewish ancestry. He was 37 years old when he fled from Germany with his wife in 1936. In Norwich he found a job in a firm distributing Calor Gas, and adopted local customs, playing football and supporting Norwich City: he used to travel to away games in his Austin Seven!

Unfortunately his stay was to be short lived. Although welcomed on a local level, he was a victim of national Government policies. Once war broke out between Germany and Britain in 1939, German nationals were regarded with suspicion and liable to internment and deportation: these citizens of Germany included not only Nazi sympathisers but also people who had actually come to this country as refugees from the Nazi regime. In October 1939, Eichenberg was brought before a Tribunal, where the case against him included letters he had written to his wife's brother in France which appeared to include a code – actually the two were simply playing a game of postal chess using standard chess notation! Eichenberg was interned in camp and then sent off to Canada with other German and Italian citizens and they travelled on the Arandora Star. On 2 July 1940, the ship was sunk by a German submarine with the loss of 700 lives. Eichenberg was one of the survivors who were brought back to England, but this was not the end of his story. They were put on board another ship, the Dunera, and after a voyage of over 50 days in terrible conditions – personal belongings were taken from them and not restored, despite Eichenberg's protests – they were interned in Australia. After the war Eichenberg, not surprisingly, did not choose to return to Norwich, emigrating to the United States in 1946, adopting the name Frank Eaton and becoming professor of German at Portland State University.

In spite of such individual tragedies, Norwich can be proud of her share in Britain's welcoming of Jewish refugees, part of the contribution recognised by the Jewish Chronicle in 1951: 'It has long been England's policy to give asylum to refugees, and its hospitality has enabled them to make their contribution to the stream of British culture'.

When Germany invaded Poland in 1939, some Poles fled to try and continue the struggle against the enemy. Unable to cross Germany, they headed south over the Carpathian mountains, through Hungary and Yugoslavia and then travelled either by sea or overland across Italy to France. Many served in the Air Force there. When France was defeated in 1940, those who could came to Britain, some serving in Norfolk airbases. To them, Britain was the last place in Europe from which they could conduct their fight against the Nazi regime. They gave it a nickname that many refugee groups may also have felt in their hearts: to these Polish refugees, Britain was Last-Hope Island.

LAST-HOPE ISLAND

Polish pilots played a vital role in the winning of the Battle of Britain, a turning point in the war against Germany. Men from other conquered countries also came to Norfolk to continue the fight, including men from Czechoslovakia, Norway and France. There were also men from many Commonwealth countries serving in the area, and some who died in Norwich or nearby are buried in Earlham cemetery. They include John Sheridan (Australian) and Wilfred Cameron, (Canadian), killed at Hellesdon on 31 May 1942, and Robert Kater and James Lemon (both Canadian) and Colin Barton (New Zealander), who died together in a crash on Mousehold Heath on 25 July 1942. Another airman's grave remembers David Taylor, from South Africa and a Jew: he was a professor at the Royal Academy of Music and died on 23 November 1941. Buried nearby in the cemetery are four German airmen, killed when their plane crashed at Poringland on 9 May 1942: men from so many nationalities are brought together here in death.

The group of soldiers who had most effect in Norwich was that of the American Army Air Force, which had many bases in the area, and whose soldiers shopped and socialised in the city. The American air force bases around Norfolk were a dramatic feature of wartime life, remembered by many local people: the nearest was at Horsham St Faith, now the city's international airport, from where men could easily walk or cycle into the city to shop, enjoy an English tea or a beer, or dance at the *Samson and Hercules* or the *Lido*. Others would come from bases further away, the trucks bringing them into the city were known as 'Liberty Runs'. Many of these American airmen were themselves the sons or grandsons of immigrants, such as Leo Reovulus, whose father had emigrated to the United States from Lithuania, where he was a coal miner by trade. A number were themselves immigrants, such as Ludwig Lund, born in Odense, Denmark in 1908. His family emigrated in 1920 when Lund was 12, and in the war he found himself back in Europe, where he served as the official Army Illustrator of the Second Air Division, painting scenes both of air force activity and of scenes in Norfolk and Norwich.

The Americans were better paid than the English, and many Norwich people who were children during the war still recall their generosity. In 1943, they used Carrow Road football stadium to host a rodeo! At the time the war broke out there were men of many origins in the American Army Air Force, including Europeans, Mexicans and native Americans, but no Afro-Americans. This changed during the war and black people were among the Americans in the Norwich area, some acting as support staff on air bases, others in the gathering army preparing for D-Day, such as those in the camp on the site of the present-day County Hall and Record Office. The American army practised segregation and black soldiers had their own units, and also their own places where they tended to gather when off duty: the *Duke of Connaught* pub on the Prince of Wales Road was one such place. For many Norwich people, these were the first black persons that they had seen. Norwich can be proud of the reaction of one local woman, as recorded in the wartime diaries of Rachel Dhonau (herself of German extraction): on one occasion, some white American soldiers loudly refused to eat in a local restaurant because of the presence of a number of black soldiers. 'One Norwich woman stood up and said that if they were good enough to fight they were good enough to mix with'. The identity of this feisty lady is unknown, but she embodies the spirit of welcome that this book celebrates.

Other incomers were not here by choice. As David Jones recalled – 'there were two prisoner of war camps in Norwich, one German and one Italian. I can remember the Germans playing football against some of our boys up on Duchy's [a field off Ranworth Road]... The Germans didn't speak to you much, but the Italians were allowed to go and help round the houses. We had an Italian help with our garden – he would eat with us and then go back to the camp in the evening'.

Many people in Britain have themselves been refugees, although under a different name. During the Second World War several million children were moved away from cities, usually with their school groups and teachers rather than their parents. These children all have stories to tell of their reception by strangers – many were made very welcome, others treated very badly. Norwich was thought a place likely to be bombed, so children

American airmen play basketball in front of Elison memorials in Blackfriars' Hall.

were not sent there in 1939, but this soon changed. The blitz of 1940 and the V1 and V2 rockets of June 1944 led to many houses being destroyed in London and made many families refugees: these families also found themselves 'strangers in a strange land' – the countryside of England. In the summer of 1944, there were over 20,000 such refugees in the Norwich area. On one day in July alone, over 800 arrived at the railway station, the youngest just two weeks old! All were found accommodation of some kind, the lucky ones with families or in empty houses, the less fortunate were put up in Nissen huts, sometimes without water or electricity.

The experiences of refugees and those who cared for them during the war gave rich and poor, townsfolk and country-folk a new understanding of how other people lived. Many people acted with extraordinary generosity, such as the proprietors of the Hippodrome Theatre in Norwich, which put on pantomimes and other events for evacuee children, refugee children welcomed into the community. The Hippodrome was bombed during the war: two Danish immigrants were killed, Anders Pederson, the trainer of a troupe of sea-lions performing at the theatre, and his wife, Dagmar.

AFTERWARDS

The war in Europe ended in May 1945, but for many refugees in the city this was not the end. Most of the children on the Kindertransporte never saw their parents again as they were victims of the gas chambers. Fuchel was fortunate, his parents had managed to escape to France, but the long separation brought its own problems as he recalled: 'my parents let go of a seven-year-old and got back a 16-year-old. And my mother, especially, wanted to carry on where she'd left off. And a 16-year-old doesn't like to be treated like a seven-year-old'. Fuchel acknowledged how fortunate he was compared to many, not only had he found his parents but the Cohens of Norwich had become like another set of parents to him. Hertha Fischer was one of several of the group who chose to stay in Norwich after the war was over, remaining in the city for her entire life.

It was several years before the prisoners of war could return to their homes. They were still in camp in the bitter winter of 1947 and many local people remember seeing them helping clear the snow off street pavements. Not all made it home – Wilhelm Gilbert, a German sailor died in Mousehold Camp on 27 September 1946, while another sailor at the Camp, Willi Nellison, was killed clearing mines on Horsey Beach on 20 January 1947. A few of the prisoners chose to stay on in the city after the war. One was Salvatore Rea, an Italian prisoner of war who arrived in England in 1943: after his release he worked on farms in Drayton and Hellesdon.

It is well known that quite a large number of local girls married American servicemen and emigrated with them to the United States. There were also cases where the couple decided to stay on in Norwich. Others returned later, such as Frank Pedrick Farnum, of the United States Army Air Force, who came back in the 1960s to live in Norwich with his British-born wife. At the end of the war, the airmen themselves started a fund to create a memorial to the 7,000 young Americans who had lost their lives flying from bases in East Anglia: the Second Air Division Memorial Library in Norwich continues to develop cultural and social links between Norfolk and the United States.

The wartime generation of Polish men and women were doubly unfortunate – the Nazi regime was defeated only to be replaced by a Stalinist regime equally impossible for many of them to endure. Hence a large number of Poles stayed on in Britain as welcome refugees from tyranny at home. During the war, many Polish pilots were based at Coltishall, north of Norwich, and they continued to operate from here as the Second World War turned into the Cold War. Some made the ultimate

Memorial at St Andrew's Hospital to members of the Polish community.

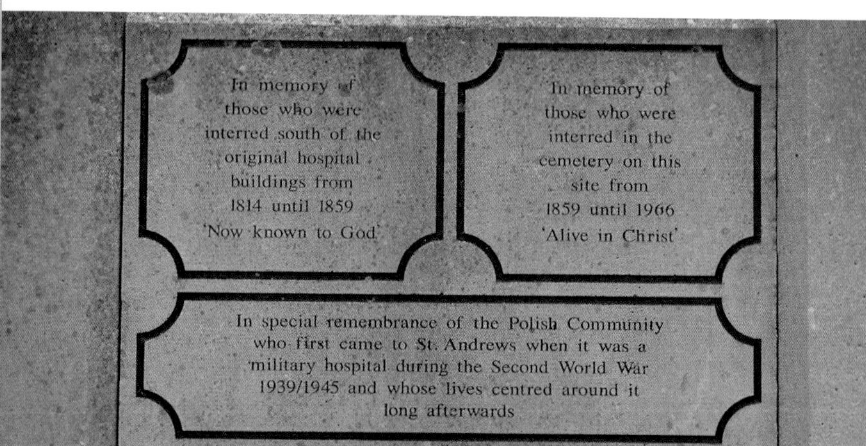

Eugenia's grave,
Earlham Cemetery.

sacrifice. If you continue down the Earlham Road to the Cemetery, you can see a group of Polish graves. They include Kasimierz Socha, one of those who stayed in Norfolk after the war had ended: he was killed in a flying accident in March 1946. If you look at the graves you may notice that one is of a female, one of only two graves of Polish women air force personnel in Britain. This is of Eugenia Zagajewska. Born in Ostrow in Poland in 1924, she was working as a secretary for the Polish Air Force in the war, based at their HQ in London. She spent Easter weekend in 1946 with a girl friend who was based at Coltishall airbase. Eugenia's fiancé, Wladzislaw Slizewski, a Polish sailor based in Scotland, also stayed with them. They were Roman Catholics and Easter Monday was a holiday for them after worship on Good Friday and Easter Sunday, so the three young Poles went from Coltishall airbase to Lamas for an afternoon's boating, using a plane's fuel tank. The 'boat' upset and Eugenia and Wladzislaw drowned in each other's arms, both were just 21 years old. They are buried in Earlham Cemetery, a thousand miles from their homeland.

Quite a number of the Poles were patients at St Andrew's Hospital, and this continued to be a social centre for the community for many years. This is remembered in a plaque on the site of the Hospital's burial ground, and in a nearby memorial to one individual, Hipolit Zaniewski (1912-1997). The plaque recalls 'the Polish community who first came to St Andrews when it was a military hospital during the Second World War 1939/1945 and whose lives centred around it long afterwards'. These refugees are also remembered in a plaque in the Cathedral, on the left as you walk towards the high altar. It reads (in English and in Polish):

> *In memory of those who died and in thanksgiving from those Poles who found hearth and home here.*

CHAPTER 14

The Later 20th Century

Sport has continued to transcend nationality, with sporting heroes from all over the world gracing the city stage. Motor cycle speedway was very popular in the city, the stadium at the Firs opening in 1930. Speedway embraced internationalism long before football did; the city's most famous rider was the Swede Ove Fundin, who rode for Norwich Stars between 1955 and 1964. Known as the 'Flying Fox' from the colour of his hair, he was world champion four times between 1956 and 1963 while he was at Norwich, and again in 1967. Other international stars to give pleasure to many thousands of spectators at the Firs included Swede Olle Nygren and Australian Aub Lawson. Another Australian, Max Grossktreutz was the team's manager in the years before the Second World War.

Opposite: Justin Fashanu, football hero, 1979.

NORWICH CITY FOOTBALL CLUB

Norwich City Football Club has welcomed heroes from many nations. Perhaps the most interesting of their many star players was Justin Fashanu. Fashanu was the son of a Nigerian barrister living in England. After his parents split up, he and his brother John went to a Doctor Barnardo's Home and then to foster parents at Shropham near Attleborough. He became an apprentice at Norwich City, turning professional in December 1978. In three years he made 90 appearances and scored 35 goals: he also won 11 England Under-21 caps. In August 1981, he became Britain's first £1million black footballer when he was bought for Nottingham Forest by manager Brian Clough. His career stalled at this point, and he played for many lesser clubs over the following years. It was while he was playing for Torquay that he came out as gay in an interview with the *Sun* published on 22 October 1990 and he featured on the cover of *Gay Times* in July 1991. He subsequently played for clubs in Scotland and America. On the morning of 2 May 1998, he was found hanged

Muhammad Ali in Norwich.

Ove Fundin, speedway star.

in a garage in Shoreditch; he was 37 years old. He will be remembered as the first professional footballer to say that he was gay – and for some of the most spectacular goals ever scored by the Canaries, including one against Liverpool in 1980 that was the BBC Goal of the Season. His brother John was also a star footballer, most notably at Norwich, Millwall and Wimbledon, winning one England cap.

Boxing has always been international in character. Billy Conn served with the American Air Force in Norfolk during the war, and world champion Joe Louis was an occasional visitor to the county. The most famous boxer of the later 20th century, Muhammad Ali, visited Norwich on 19 October 1971, doing a promotional event for Ovaltine at a supermarket in St Stephen's Road – a plaque was put up in 2003, but has since disappeared.

UNIVERSITY OF EAST ANGLIA

The establishment of a university for the city, the University of East Anglia (UEA), has brought many thousands of international students. Among them has been Kazuo Ishiguro, who was born in Nagasaki, Japan, in 1954, the family moving to England in 1960. He was at the UEA in 1979-80, obtaining an MA in creative writing, and became a UK citizen in 1982. His books include *The Remains of the Day*, which won the Booker Prize on its publication in 1989 and was filmed in 1982, *The Unconsoled* (1995) and *When We Were Orphans* (2000).

There have been distinguished incomers on the staff of the university as well, such as German-born writer W G Sebald. Sebald ('Max' to his friends) was born in Bavaria in 1944. He worked at the UEA as professor of Modern German Literature, from 1970. His classic works including *The Rings of Saturn* and *Austerlitz*, were written in Norfolk. He died in a car crash in 2001 aged 57. *The Rings of Saturn*, set around the East Anglian coast, uses the coastline as an emblem of continual change and the impermanence of all things – including national identities.

Another academic incomer, although not connected with the UEA, was also a short term resident of the city, in this case spending the last period of her life in retirement at the Great Hospital: Marietta Pallis. Born in Greece, she was a pioneering female scientist of the early 20th century who broke through many barriers to achieve this status. She conducted pioneering ecological field research on the Norfolk Broads from 1908, studying aquatic vegetation in river valleys of East Norfolk and publishing on that topic in 1911. Her practical experience in digging an island in the shape of a double-headed eagle in the Broads was of great use to Joyce Lambert in the 1950s, when she was asserting that the Broads were man-made peat diggings (and not naturally-formed lakes), an opinion now universally accepted. Marietta lived near Hickling for many years and is buried there on a floating reed bed with her partner, Phyllis Clark.

Another female immigrant to grace the city was Bianca Sforza, Italian-born sculptress who lived in Norwich until her death in 1993. Her city class was attended by another important figure in the world of sculpture, Carla Sirilli.

FOOD

Many recent incomers into the city have brought their own shops and restaurants, beginning with the first Chinese restaurant in about 1960. Five years later there were already three on Prince of Wales Road alone, and there were at least half a dozen in the city by 1970. They had been joined by an Indian restaurant (the Taj Mahal), an Italian one (Spaghettiland) and an

The first Chinese restaurant in the city, opened in the early 1960s.

American import – a Wimpy Bar. When architectural historian Sir Nikolaus Pevsner visited the city he came across a cafe boasting foot-long frankfurters. Ordering one, he measured it to find it was an inch short of the claim. (Pevsner himself was a Jewish refugee from Nazi Germany: his 'Buildings of England' series are a unique contribution to an understanding of buildings, including those of Norwich).

Over the last decades of the century, the international range of eating and drinking places has become enormous as the city has welcomed incomers from all over the globe. Rationing continued well after the war, and people turned to more exotic food in their cooking as the age of austerity came to an end. This was helped by the rise of the supermarket and the increasing range of goods that it offered – a typical store had 4,000 products in 1970, but 23,000 products three decades later.

FAITH

Many immigrants have found their own faith being practised in the city, and this can act as a great support, just as it did for the Protestant refugees of five centuries ago. Most members of the Italian community were Roman Catholic, as were many of the Polish community living in the city after the war. In the 1960s, many nurses from the Philippines were invited into Britain to fill up shortages in National Health Service hospitals. A large number of these groups came together to worship in the Cathedral of St John the Baptist, and the church has continued to provide support for newer groups of immigrants: a regular service is held in Polish at the church. Other faith groups have also welcomed believers from across the world.

The mosque in Norwich is unusual in that it was originally founded by English converts to the religion rather than incomers. Ian Dallas converted to Islam after visiting Marrakesh in the 1960s, he took the name Abdalqadir after the 12th century saint and scholar. He founded a community in Wood Dalling Hall but moved to Norwich in 1977 when the building on Chapelfield East, formerly St Peter's school, became available. In the same year an Egyptian business man visited the mosque and gave it support on condition that it was named in honour of his mother, Ihsan. It developed links with a mosque in Brixton, from which a number of Muslims of largely West Indian origin, moved to Norwich. It has also provided a centre of faith to the increasing number of Muslims living and working in Norwich, or studying at the University.

Non-believers too can equally share in the width and variety of experience that incomers bring, and take pride in the way in which the city's tradition of welcoming refugees over the generations has continued into the 21st century and resulted in formal recognition of Norwich as a city of refuge.

LANGUAGE

We have already seen that the word 'gate' in Norwich street names is from the Scandinavian tongue. Other words from the language still in use today include the place name 'Thorpe', meaning an outlying settlement, and 'staithe', the word Norwich and Norfolk people use for a landing stage on the river. The Dutch made their contribution too. Have you ever wondered why open spaces in Norwich are called Plains rather than Squares? This is another word brought over by refugees, in this case the Dutch word 'plein', meaning 'open space'. Other Dutch words taken into Norfolk speech include 'dwile' meaning floor-cloth and 'fye', meaning 'to clean': the name Fye Bridge may come from this word.

The large windows to the upper floors of houses, introduced by weavers to provide as much light as possible onto their looms, are known in Norfolk as 'lucams'. The word is taken directly from the French word 'lucarnes'.

One of the best-known aspects of Norfolk dialect is the habit of dropping the 's' of the third person singular of the present tense. Norfolk people often say 'he go' rather than 'he goes' and 'she love' rather than 'she loves him'. Language expert Peter Trudgill suggests this shows the influence of the incomers of the 16th century.

THE MYSTERIOUS MORAY-SMITH

One local artist who has given pleasure to many Norwich residents is the man whose name is generally given as John Moray-Smith. He worked for Morgan's Brewery from the 1930s, and created many of the city's most striking pieces of art, such as the plaques inside the *Woolpack*, the wall-art outside the *Prince of Denmark*, and the two plaques illustrating life in medieval Norwich on the outsides of the *Coachmaker's Arms* and the *Ber Street Gates* public houses. Moray-Smith and his wife Katrin lived in Costessey for 30 years, dying within a month of each other in 1958, but almost nothing is really known about them, not even their true names. The couple appear in rate books with the surname Moray-Smith, but also with the simple surname Smith; they are supposed to have met at the Slade Art School, but their names are not in the School's records. Reminiscences of friends and neighbours persistently hint at immigrant origins, some suggesting Belgian, others Polish (for Katrin at least): the most commonly accepted tradition is that he was born in Italy, his work in plasterwork continuing those of 19th century predecessors in the medium whom we have already considered. It is a tribute to the internationalism of today's Norwich that we can appreciate these works of art without knowing the nationality of their creator: does it even really matter?

Moray-Smith's work on the *Prince of Denmark* and *Ber Street Gates* public houses.

Saint George and the dragon,
St George Tombland church.
Right: Saint George and the dragon,
St Gregory's church.

ENGLAND AND SAINT GEORGE

Saint George has become the national saint of England and a symbol of national pride. It is ironic that among the very few things we know about George is that he had absolutely no connection with this country! He was martyred for his Christian faith in Palestine in about AD 300. It is likely that he was a soldier in the Roman Army, which included men from all parts of the Roman Empire and beyond – George could have been of any nationality!

Saint George became especially revered in Norwich: the writer Sir Walter Scott thought – wrongly – that he was actually the patron saint of the city. The best-known story about him is that he killed a dragon, and he and the dragon used to parade around the city in procession every year on Saint George's Day. This came to an end over five centuries ago, at the Reformation. However, the dragon still appears every year in the Mayor's Day procession in June. This dragon, known as Snap, is the direct descendant of the one who fought Saint George in the city processions so many years ago. Representations of the dragon, with or without Saint George are very common in the city, most notably the carving that gives us the name Dragon Hall. Two other fine images of this foreigner who has become England's national saint can be seen today in the church of St Gregory and in St George Tombland.

The Dragon Festival, held in Norwich in 2009 and 2011 continues to celebrate the role of the dragon and Saint George.

Conclusion

In the 1570s a document was drawn up by the city authorities listing the benefits that the Strangers had brought to Norwich over the previous ten years: it is now among the National Archives. They are worth recalling today:

1 They brought a great commodity thither, namely the making of bays, moccados, grograynes, all sorts of tufts etc, which were not made there before, whereby they do not only set on work their own people but do also set on work our own people within the city as also a great number near twenty miles about the city, to the great relief of the poorer sort there.

2 By their means our city is well inhabited, and decayed houses rebuilt and repaired that were in ruin and more wolde and now good rents [paid] for the same.

3 The merchants by their commodities have and may have great trade as well within the realm as without the realm being in good estimation in all places.

4 It cannot be but whereas a number of people be but the one receive commodity of the other as well of the city as men of the country.

5 They be contributors to all payments as subsidies, tasks, watches, contributions, ministers' wages etc.

6 Our own people do practice and make such commodities as the strangers do make, whereby the youth is set to work and kept from idleness.

7 They dig and delve a number of acres of ground and do sow flax, and do make it out in linen cloth which set many in work.

8 They dig and delve a great quantity of ground for roots, which is a great succour and sustenance for the poor both for them[selves] as for all others of city and country.

9 They live wholly of themselves without charge, and do beg of no man, and do sustain all their own poor people.

10 And to conclude, they for the most part fear God, and do diligently and laboriously attend upon their several occupations, they obey all magistrates and all good laws and ordinances, they live peaceably among themselves and toward all men, and we think our city happy to enjoy them.

This was almost 500 years ago: and the same could well be said of the refugee groups in the city today. As we think about the stories of people like Felix, Herbert Losinga, Brice the Dutchman, Janus Gruter and Eugenia Zagajewska, we can begin to appreciate the contribution that has been made by immigrants to Norwich over so many centuries. The city has been twinned with Rouen in France, Koblenz in Germany and Novi Sad in

Serbia – these bonds of friendship are celebrated in street and bridge names in the city, while the contribution of incomers continues to enhance the life of the city today.

In this book we have looked at the experience of immigrants and refugees to Norwich over many centuries. Similar stories are to be found in today's city, as Norwich continues to welcome people fleeing from war, persecution or natural disasters: it is a fitting tribute to our forebears that we continue to offer sanctuary to people most in need. In the same way that refugees of Dutch, Flemish, Walloon and Huguenot origin, and people from all over the world have over the centuries become part of the city's shared identity. More recent arrivals from places such as the Democratic Republic of the Congo, Afghanistan, Iraq and Uganda continue to enrich our culture.

Their story is our story.

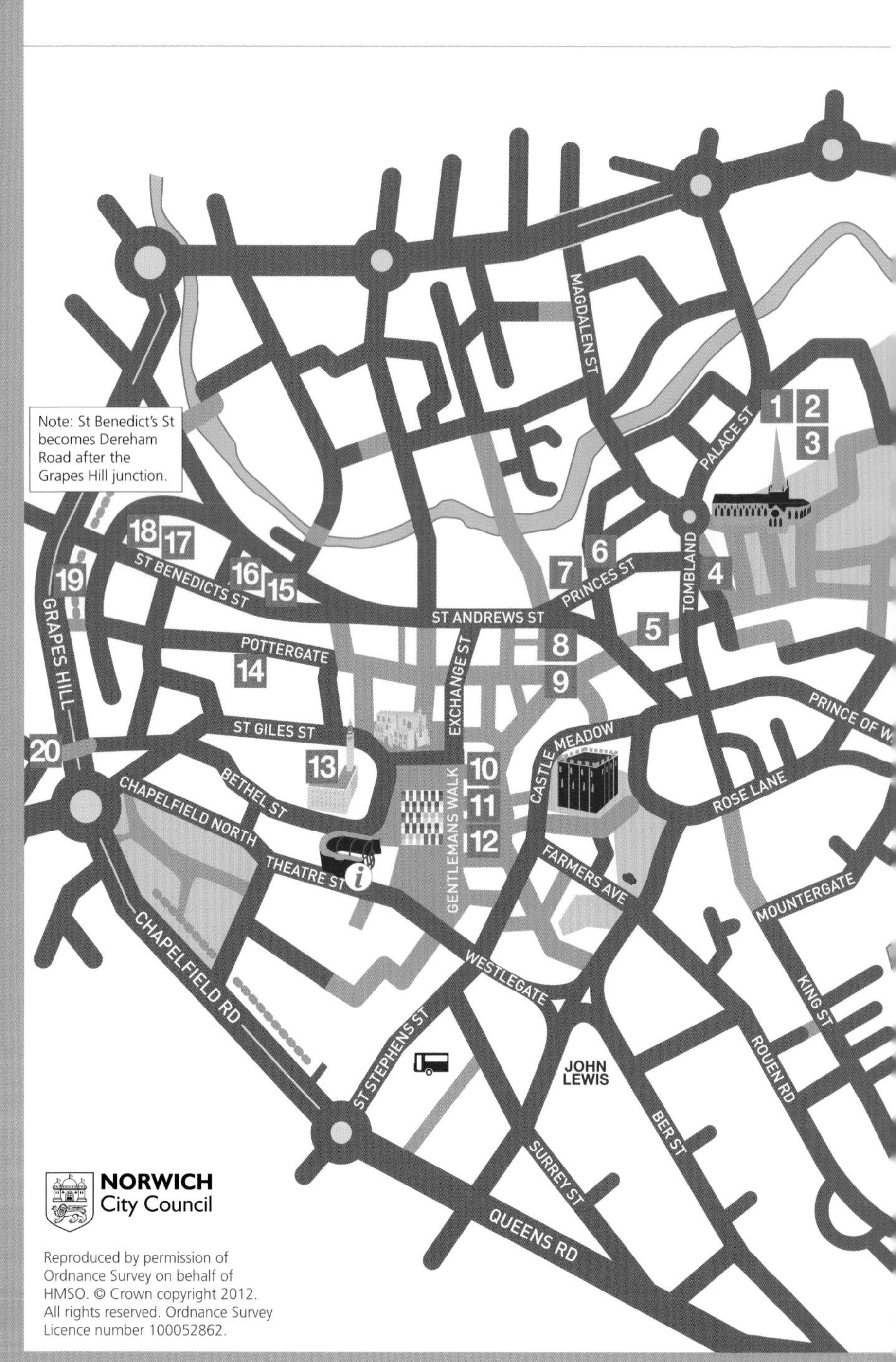

NORWICH
City Council

THE WALK

A Walk Around Norwich

Two to two and a half hours should be allowed for this walk which begins at the Anglican Cathedral and ends at the Cathedral of St John the Baptist. It can easily be divided into two walks – from the Anglican Cathedral to the Market Place and from the Market Place to the Cathedral of St John the Baptist. There are no steps (apart from those down to the entrance to St Lawrence, a detour), but the slopes are steeper than those who think of Norwich as very flat might expect! As you walk you will notice the enormous number of 'foreign' shops, cafes and restaurants' along the route: you could try counting them! Any one would make an ideal place for a break for refreshment along the way.

STOP 1

Norwich (Anglican) Cathedral
The interior of the nave is an astonishing example of Norman architecture: only the vaulted roof is more recent. Go to the far east end of the south aisle: the statue on the wall is almost certainly of Saint Felix (see page 16), born in Burgundy, who founded the diocese of East Anglia. The stained glass window beside it, showing a bishop, is European glass, originally made in Rouen: it was brought to England by the German merchant, J C Hampp.

Walk to the south west corner of the cloister.

STOP 2

The Green Man. Look at the ceiling: can you see the Green Man carving, the second boss from the entrance arch (see page 26). These bosses were carved by a Dutchman named Brice and in 1416, he was paid 4s 8d for his work (about 23p in today's money, but this of course was worth a great deal more in the 15th century). It took him two weeks to carve.

Walk into the Cathedral Close, past the refectory and herb garden.

STOP 3

Note the rounded gables on the house across the road: these are in a style brought over from the Low Countries, and known as **Dutch Gables**.

Walk straight on through the Ethelbert Gate and stand just in front of it.

STOP 4

This is **Tombland**: this was the Market Place at the heart of the Saxon town, with main roads running into it from all directions (that to the east has been blocked by the Norman Cathedral). The name itself is from a Scandinavian word meaning 'empty ground' – nothing to do with tombs.

Looking through the archway beside the gate you can see a red brick building with 'S'-shaped tiles, known as pantiles – another Dutch import. The building is on the **site of the Franciscan friary**: Peter of Candia was a friar here – he later became Pope Alexander V.

Cross the road and walk up Queen Street. Stop at the iron gates on your right.

STOP 5

The French Church. On your right you will find the church of St Mary the Less, one of several Norwich parish churches closed at the Reformation. It was used as a hall for Strangers' goods until 1637 when it became the church of French-speaking refugees from the Low Countries – Walloons. At the end of the 17th century they were joined by Protestant refugees from France – the Huguenots. There are monuments inside to the Martineau and Colombine families.

Walk on to the top of Queen Street.

STOP 6

The Church of St Michael at Plea. There are monuments inside to the de Hem family, one of the richest merchant families among the 16th century. The most noticeable is to Anna, who died in childbirth in 1603. The large white building beside the churchyard was the Bally and Haldinstein shoe factory: Philip Haldinstein was an immigrant from Germany.

Turn right and walk down the hill past Cinema City, stop at St Andrew's Plain.

STOP 7

The Halls. This stunning building was built by Black Friars, followers of the Spanish Saint Dominic. The east part (Blackfriars' Hall) was used as its church by the Dutch-speaking community. There are monuments inside to John Elison and his son Theophilus, both pastors to the community.

Cross the road and walk up St Andrew's Hill with the church on your right.

STOP 8

6 St Andrew's Hill. This is where the Lazarus family lived a century ago: they were Jewish refugees from Poland who worked here as tailors. The small doorway to the right is the entrance to the Bridewell: Samuel Turner, a native of Martinique in the West Indies would have been brought through here, dying in the Bridewell in 1819. Further up the hill at 2 St Andrew's Hill see the weavers' windows on the second floor which are known as lucams, a word taken from the French.

Walk on into London Street, stopping at the circular bench.

STOP 9

London Street. To your right, just off London Street, is the *Wild Man* public house, named after an immigrant from Germany who was in the Bridewell in the 1750s. On London Street, opposite the signpost, note the plaque to Louis Marchesi: this is where the first meetings of the Round Table were held.

Walk down London Street and along Castle Street.

STOP 10

Davey Place. Here we can see the key features of the Norman town, the Market Place and the Norwich Castle upon its mound.

Continue past the Royal Arcade and the entrance to the shopping mall.

STOP 11

White Lion Street. This was one of the main streets in the medieval Jewry: if you look at page 20, you can see the names of some of the people who lived here and their occupations: note the herb garden!

Walk down White Lion Street, away from the shopping mall entrance and at the end turn left onto Haymarket.

STOP 12

Haymarket. The medieval Jewish synagogue stood opposite the Haymarket, where among other sculptures is the statue is of Thomas Browne. He was an international figure, like many students of today – he was educated at Montpelier in France and Leiden in the Netherlands. To the right is St Peter Mancroft church where three African boys, freed slaves, were baptised in the church font in 1813. In the church is a fine Flemish tapestry (see page 50).

Walk up towards The Forum, turn right and go to the main entrance of City Hall.

STOP 13

The bronze doors of City Hall have plaques showing scenes of the city's history: can you spot that of the Vikings coming up the river?

Continue past City Hall and cross the road. Go and down to the bottom of Upper Goat Lane, which is left of Lower Goat Lane.

STOP 14

You are at the crossing of two of the roads in Norwich containing the Scandinavian element 'gata'. The road you are crossing is **Pottergate**, Upper Goat Lane, down which you have just walked used to be called Stonegate. Note the plaques to your left on the building of the Society of Friends: they commemorate Elizabeth Fry and Thomas Fowell Buxton, local people who played important parts in the abolition of slavery, and worked in support of people like Olaudah Equiano.

Cross the green space in front of St Gregory's church and walk underneath the arch beneath the chancel of the church onto the main road.

STOP 15

The Hog and Armour public house. You are on the line of the Roman road running east-west across the city. This is where that road was crossed by another running south-north: the shape of the urban landscape here is that laid out by immigrants from Rome two thousand years ago.

STOP 16

Next to the pub is **Strangers' Hall**. The origin of the name is not certain. It was in the hands of Nicholas Sotherton who as we have seen was friendly to the Strangers of the 16th century, and who may perhaps have welcomed some into some part of his home. A baptism entry in the Dutch church in 1604 refers to a little Dutch girl as born 'in Xenodochio': this is a Greek word meaning 'a place for strangers' and has been taken to mean Strangers' Hall. The words 'Strangers' Hall' are used in the city archives; what is actually being talked about is St Mary the Less, the Hall where the Strangers conducted their business. Leonard Bolingboke, the man who preserved Strangers' Hall and gave it to the city thought it came much later, from the time in the early 19th century when it

6 Valentine Street – surgery of the Indian oculists in 1893 (Stop 19).

was occupied by immigrants and refugees like D'Etreville and Mazzotti.

Turn back and continue along St Benedict's, following the line of the Roman road.

STOP 17

9 St Benedict's Street. This house was occupied by three generations of the Ecker family, refugees from Poland who established a tailoring business here, which flourished and employed several local workers.

Continue along St Benedict's Street, following the line of the Roman road.

STOP 18

St Lawrence church. If you go halfway down the steps at the lower end of the church, you can see a medieval image of Vikings as they are engaged in murdering Saint Edmund! This church contains the monument to John Asger, who was in Bruges when he was called back to become mayor of Norwich.

Continue along St Benedict's Street and across the major road junction into Dereham Road. Turn first left, up Valentine Street.

STOP 19

6 Valentine Street. This is the house where the Indian oculists practised in 1893, curing the blindness of several local people with the knowledge of medicine that they brought with them.

Walk up the hill, either beside Grapes Hill or through the flats and up Paragon Place.

STOP 20

The Cathedral of St John the Baptist. Inside, the rood screen is the work of a German artist, Peter Rendl. One of the images at the east end of the cathedral is of Saint Felix, born in Burgundy and recognised as the founder of Christianity in East Anglia by both cathedrals. As you walk down the north aisle, note the plaque put up in honour of Polish immigrants of an earlier generation, such as Eugenia Zagajewska. This is a good place to remember both the sacrifice and the contribution made by immigrants to Norwich over the centuries: in the words of the document the city sent to the Privy Council 500 years ago, 'we think our city happy to enjoy them'.

The walk ends. Cross the pedestrian overpass onto Upper St Giles Street which leads into St Giles Street to take you back to the city centre.

PICTURE CREDITS

Thanks are due to many institutions for kind permission to use the illustrations within this book. These include:

Photographs © June 2012 **Museum of Fine Arts, Boston**: Page 34: Rembrandt Harmensz. van Rijn, Dutch, 1606–1669. *Reverend Johannes Elison*, 1634. Oil on canvas. 174.0x124.5cm (68.5x49in.) Museum of Fine Arts, Boston William K. Richardson Fund, 56.510

Page 54: Rembrandt Harmensz. van Rijn, Dutch, 1606–1669. *Mevr. Johannes Elison*, 1634 Oil on canvas. 174.9x124.1cm (68 7/8 x 48 7/8 in.) Museum of Fine Arts, Boston William K. Richardson Fund, 56.511

Collection: **Tasmanian Museum and Art Gallery**: Page 66: John Dempsey. *Cotton, A Black, Norwich* watercolour. Presented by Mr. C.E. Docker, 1956 AG567.

Page 70: John Dempsey. *Black Charley, Bootmaker, Norwich* 1823 watercolour. Presented by Mr. C.E. Docker, 1956. AG574.

Norfolk Libraries, Picture Norfolk:
Page 88: Norwich Synagogue.
Page 96: Pietro Chiesa.
Images courtesy of Norfolk County Council Library and Information Service – enjoy thousands of images of Norfolk's unique history at www.picture.norfolk.gov.uk

Norfolk Museums and Archaeology Service:
Page 19: Elizabeth Fry, 1835, CR Leslie.
© Norfolk Museums and Archaeology Service (Norwich Castle Museum and Art Gallery).
Page 78: John Theodore Heins Sr *Self Portrait* 1726, oil on copper. NWHCM : 1974.462.
© Norfolk Museums and Archaeology Service (Norwich Castle Museum and Art Gallery).
Page 79: Dutch School *View of Norwich* c.1707, oil on deal panel. NWHCM : 1967.341.
© Norfolk Museums and Archaeology Service (Norwich Castle Museum and Art Gallery).

ITV Anglia and East Anglian Film Archive:
Page 99: Anna Hannent.
Page 116: Muhammad Ali.
Page 117: Ove Fundin.

Andi Sapey:
Pages 16, 26, 50, 121.

George Plunkett:
Page 87: St Giles', Tuck's Court [0344] 1934-12-26.

Norfolk Record Office:
Page 20 [NRS 20676].
Page 22 [DCN 40/1].
Page 23 [NRS 20673].
Page 39 [NCR 17d].
Page 40 [NCR 17d].
Page 57 [N/MC 1/12].
Page 58 [MC 257/1].
Page 74 [NNH 93/34].
Page 84 [MS 177].
Page 83 [BOL6/36].
Page 92 [N/AR UNCAT].
Page 100 [BR 122/98/1].
Page 118 [ACC 2007/318].

American Memorial Library
(held at the Norfolk Record Office):
Page 104 [MC 376/599]: Ludwig Lund's daughter, Mrs M Lund-Fontaine has kindly given her permission to use her father's painting.

Page 102 and 103: Images from the Carrow Works Magazine, January 1915.

Other photographs belong to the author Frank Meeres and Norwich HEART.
The photograph of Justin Fashanu on page 114 comes from a Norwich City Football Club programme.

FURTHER READING

V D Lipman *The Jews of Medieval Norwich* (1967).

W J C Moens *The Walloons and their church in Norwich* (1887-8). This is still the starting-point for those researching their 'Stranger' ancestry.

Raingard Esser *Norwich Strangers Book 1583-1600* (1990), and other articles and booklets by this author.

Frank Meeres *The Story of Norwich* (2011).

Ian Robinson and Annemarie Young, *Gervelie's Journey* (2008). The true story of a refugee coming to Norwich, as told by a child.

Nick Williams *The Blue Plaques of Norwich* (2010).

Mike Loveday *The Norwich Knowledge* (2011).

ACKNOWLEDGEMENTS

The author would like to express his thanks for the support and help of Norwich HEART and the Norfolk Record Office (County Archivist, Dr John Alban). Many individuals have also contributed: they include Victoria Draper, Kevin Holmwood, Nick Little, Louise Watling, Ian Williams, Michael Loveday, Nick Williams and Sophie Cabot.

INDEX

Opposite: The Low Countries, showing the main places from which the Strangers came to Norwich. Source: A W Moore, Dutch and Flemish Painting in Norfolk (1988).